NEVER TRUMP

Why Obsessional Elites Are Undermining
the Future of America

NEVER TRUMP

Why Obsessional Elites Are Undermining
the Future of America

RICHARD KRADIN, MD.

DEFIANCE PRESS
& PUBLISHING

Never Trump: Why Obsessional Elites Are Undermining the Future of America

Printed in the United States of America

10 9 8 7 6 5 4 3 2 1

DEFIANCE PRESS
& PUBLISHING

ISBN-13: 978-1-948035-71-2 (Paperback)
ISBN-13: 978-1-948035-72-9 (ebook)

Edited by Janet Musick
Cover designed by Spomenka Bojanic
Interior designed by Debbi Stocco

Published by Defiance Press and Publishing, LLC

Bulk orders of this book may be obtained by contacting Defiance Press and Publishing, LLC. www.defiancepress.com.

Public Relations Dept. – Defiance Press & Publishing, LLC
281-581-9300
pr@defiancepress.com

Defiance Press & Publishing, LLC
281-581-9300
info@defiancepress.com

Acknowledgements

I dedicate this book to S. Thanks for listening to my daily rants about the state of the nation and the workplace. It is no country for old men.

I am indebted to Janet Musick for her professional excellence and attention to detail in editing this text. My thanks also to Heather Siler for her support in bringing this text to public attention.

TABLE OF CONTENTS

Table of Contents

A PERSONAL PREFACE

I grow old...I grow old. I shall wear
the bottoms of my trousers rolled.
　　　— T.S. Eliot, The Love Song of J. Alfred Prufrock

Since the first printing of this text, the country has witnessed a seemingly endless series of efforts by Progressive Democrats and Conservative "Never Trump!" Republicans to rid the country of the 45th president by any means necessary. These have included efforts to change the Electoral College, discredited investigation into collusion of the Trump campaign with Russia, an unsuccessful impeachment campaign, a steadfast resistance to all of the Trump domestic and foreign policies, and a concerted effort by the mainstream media and "Big Tech" to censor Trump and his supporters. Their last-ditch effort has been a *second* unconstitutional impeachment of Trump based on claims that he incited an "insurrection."

The recent razor-thin margin of the highly contested November 2020 presidential election has left nearly half the country questioning the legitimacy of President Biden. Systematic changes in how ballots were cast and counted occurred at the insistence of anti-Trump partisans.

Critical information about the Biden family's business ventures were suppressed by the mainstream media and by "Big Tech." Numerous claims of voter fraud were attested to but never seriously reviewed by the courts. As a consequence, on January 20, 2021, America saw the inauguration of an evidently cognitively impaired, financially corrupt, and politically compromised President Biden.

An objective review of the Trump administration's record reveals a series of remarkable achievements that benefited Americans of all stripes. Despite this, his opponents refused to recognize or credit any of Mr. Trump's numerous accomplishments. There are many reasons for the opposition to Mr. Trump. Most are based on his conservative agenda and his "America First" policy, which threatens corporate and personal profits for those embedded in the globalist economy. But for many voters in America, their negative reaction to Mr. Trump was primarily based on psychological predispositions. The term "Trump Derangement Syndrome" is not simply a glib maxim bandied about by Conservative media pundits; rather, it is a real psychiatric disorder, one characterized by distortions of reality, fixed ideas, and intense negative feelings. Unfortunately, a good percentage of Americans suffer from it. This text aims at elucidating the psychological underpinnings of the "Trump Derangement Syndrome" that swept America for the last four years.

On a personal note, watching the protests and violence on our streets in the summer of 2020 was like déjà vu for me. As a college student in the late '60s and early '70s, like many of my peers, I espoused Progressive ideas, and participated in the massive rallies against the Vietnam war in Washington, D.C. and on Wall Street. I recall being confronted, sometimes violently, by angry working-class Americans who viewed these demonstrations as unpatriotic, and despite my youthful idealism, I too was uncomfortable with some of the radical factions that were participating in these protests. They were angrier than most others, and more willing to engage in hostile confrontations with the police. These groups included angry, privileged white men, radical feminists and black revolutionaries, whose hatred and grievances against America struck me as extreme and not supported by facts. Although disillusioned with America's positions on the war, I was not a revolutionary, and did not hate my country.

After graduating from university, I attended medical school and raised a family. The war was over and my attention was diverted away from politics. From what I could observe, the country was making progress with respect to social justice issues. Women were being accepted in the workplace, and it was rare to encounter anyone who openly expressed racist ideas. There had been substantial genuine progress.

As medicine is a time-consuming profession, much of my adult experience centered around my work. When I began training in medicine in the early 1970s, the profession was still a "men's club." Overt competition, barbed comments, outbursts by angry surgeons (then the accepted prima donnas of the medical profession), and barbed criticisms were commonplace. Racism and anti-Semitism were still evident in some quarters, although rarely openly discussed. These behaviors were unpleasant but, as medicine is an arduous profession, harsh "military-like" training was deemed appropriate. Most responded by working harder to improve their performance; those who could not handle the pressure chose to drop out. Medical training was also hierarchical, and criticisms were invariably directed "down" at trainees, while the staff was largely immune to scrutiny.

By the 1980s, the number of women graduating from medical schools had increased dramatically, and the "old boy" approach was no longer judged acceptable. Training was profoundly influenced by the presence of women, and it soon became less competitive, more relational, gentler, and permissive. The hospital staff was now reticent to criticize trainees, especially if it might leave a young female trainee in tears.

The traditional hierarchy was breaking down, and even reversing itself. Trainees were now encouraged to anonymously evaluate the medical staff. While some of these evaluations were constructive, others were blisteringly critical, vindictive and, in many instances, undeserved. If a staff member justifiably issued a less-than-enthusiastic evaluation of a trainee's performance — and these evaluations were *not* anonymous — they learned to expect a harsh evaluation in return from the trainee. Reluctant to have their reputations besmirched, staff members chose to issue glowing evaluations of *all* trainees, irrespective of their level of performance. "Grade inflation" became so exaggerated that hospital administrators needed to caution their staff that were it to continue, federal funding for medical education might justifiably be cut, as the argument could be made that trainees were *so* accomplished that they required no additional education.

Eventually, criticism of all types was viewed as "harsh" or "mean-spirited." The heightened sensitivities of trainees by the late 1980s and 1990s were so great as to render them fragile. While in the past, trainees would eagerly compete with each other to answer a question posed to them by a staff member, they were now reticent to do so. Teaching devolved into a didactic exercise rather than a dialectical one. Trainees were reluctant to admit there were things they did not know, so they simply stopped inquiring or feigned knowledge.

I attributed what was transpiring to the narcissistic fragility that was being reported in the 1980s by psychologists and societal critics (Lasch, 1979). But disturbing as was the near-uniform failure of the staff to take any constructive action to confront what was occurring, they were unwilling to support colleagues who were being unfairly threatened by entitled students. The bad behavior of students was consistently ignored unless it negatively affected them. Concern and courage were in short supply.

The following example illustrates what was transpiring. Trainees are meant to go through a standard ritual in evaluating a new patient. They are expected to take a medical history, perform a physical examination, formulate their opinions, and then present them to a senior staff physician for feedback. A few years ago, a highly intelligent but clearly self-centered young resident presented a patient to me on rounds while at the bedside. But it quickly became evident that the patient in the bed was *not* the one he was describing. In truth, he had neither seen nor examined the patient, an example of egregious misconduct. Once discovered, the trainee apologized, but I remained upset, having never witnessed such behavior in my 40 years of teaching. When I raised the issue with the residency training director, he agreed that the behavior was unacceptable, but quickly added, "Well, he must have been busy; I'm sure he'll do better next time." In years past, such behavior would have resulted summarily in dismissal from the residency. Instead, no punitive action was taken, and the individual in question was eventually rewarded with a prized fellowship position and later joined the permanent medical staff. The resident in question had been a medical student at Harvard and, as I had learned during my years teaching there, they were considered an elite group to be treated as beyond reproach.

This experience was a microcosm of what was taking place in society at large. In recent years, the enabling of bad behaviors has increased. On college campuses, students are permitted to raise havoc, deny others the right to speak, and destroy public property, all without consequences. Dialogue has been replaced by vicious *ad hominem* attacks. The entire premise of liberal education, i.e., the open exchange of ideas, has been undermined — all with minimal resistance by those who *should* know better. Many teachers have chosen to leave their positions rather than continue to work under such circumstances. Others have been forced out of their jobs by trumped-up accusations of "bigotry" or "racism."

It is currently unusual for teachers to demand performance standards from students or to confront them when they are failing. Another personal anecdote illustrates this point. A few years back, I was invited to join the guest faculty of a private educational institution in California. The agreement was that I would travel there for one week each semester to teach a two-day course. The final grade required the submission of a 15-page, double-spaced paper on a topic of the student's own choice related to the course material. The papers were due within 30 days after the end of the course.

On the last day of the course, almost the entire class immediately asked for, and was granted, an extension for submissions by the administration. But almost half the class submitted their papers a full year after the course had ended. Most of these submissions were of poor quality, highly subjective, and demonstrated little objective evidence that the students had understood the course material. When I refused to enter a final grade of "A" for any of these late submissions, that decision was questioned by the students, who thought that a grade of less than an "A" was "harsh." When I responded that, because they had taken almost a year to complete the assignment, they should not expect to receive a high grade, I was politely told by the school administration that I would not be asked to return for the following year. While this had little effect on my career or my income, the experience confirmed that holding students to a standard of excellence was no longer a priority for education. Merit was no longer a standard via which students were to be judged. Today, we hear Progressive educators condemning meritocracy as evidence of "white privilege."

With the unexpected election of Donald Trump in 2016, matters only deteriorated. The country witnessed "resistance" in the form of unrelenting attacks on Trump and his supporters. This included false claims of criminal "collusion with Russia," groundless partisan impeachments by House Democrats, a devastating viral epidemic unleashed on the West by the Communist Chinese, the looting and vandalizing of statues, purportedly excused by the apparent murder of a non-violent black felon by a white policeman in Minneapolis, and a disturbing crackdown on First Amendment rights by Progressive Democrats and their allies in the press, social media, and corporate America.[1]

What should have been America's best years were uniformly degraded by Progressives and by those Republicans who shared a deep hatred of Mr. Trump. But it is virtually impossible for many of these groups to explain lucidly the *reasons* for their intense distaste for Mr. Trump.

Recently, former National Security Advisor John Bolton was discussing his "tell-all" book that criticizes Trump. I listened to the reasons for his disenchantment with the president. Paraphrasing them, Bolton argued that Trump had no ideology, was willing to negotiate with America's enemies, and was concerned only with his own re-election. While I am not a political scientist, I could discern little in Bolton's arguments that would not apply to any first-term American president. But what struck me was Bolton's ideological rigidity. Rigid ideologically positions antithetical to Bolton's were also being espoused by the Progressive left against Trump. What the Progressive left and Conservative right share in common is a rigid ideology, which invariably reflects their underlying *psychological* rigidity.

To be specific, personality rigidity characterizes three of major

---

1   This "unholy alliance" was presciently predicted by screenwriter Paddy Chayefsky in the 1976 film *Network*.

characterological disorders recognized by psychiatrists: narcissism, obsessionality, and paranoia. If a patient presented to me espousing the ideas of the Progressive left or of the Never Trump! right, I would diagnose them with overlapping elements of all three disorders. If they were severe enough to result in delusional ideation, I would properly term them as suffering from a "limited psychosis," a serious mental disorder. In truth, what some glibly refer to as "Trump Derangement Disorder" is just that, a form of psychosis based on delusional ideation and dangerous paranoia. As will be discussed, the latter is characterized by projections in which there is a misattribution of responsibility onto one's perceived enemies, something we have been witnessing daily from these groups. Claims of election interference, corruption, insurrection, etc. directed at Trump have all been demonstrated objectively to have been actions the Democratic left is guilty of!

The remainder of this text will be devoted to examining why society has arrived at a point of collective "mental illness." But what is clear is that a mental illness of this severity cannot be allowed to fester for long. It is destructive, and must be confronted and aggressively addressed.

INTRODUCTION

I'm truly sorry man's dominion,
Has broken nature's social union.
— Robert Burns, *To a Mouse*

Much has been written about the culture wars and political conflict in America, yet few have addressed the psychological factors that contribute to this divisiveness (Schwarz, 2003). America is being torn by opposing views concerning its values. As conservative political commentator Thomas Sowell argues in *Conflict of Visions*, these result from distinct visions of what constitutes the highest "good" in society (Sowell, 2007). He suggests that these visions arise subliminally and are subject to "what we sense or feel before we have constructed any systematic reasoning that could be called a theory, much less...a hypotheses to be tested against evidence." Why we value what we do ultimately is only partially known to us.

Sowell refers to two opposing visions. These can be traced to antiquity and can be seen to intensify during times of societal stress. They generate a field effect that includes perspectives on a wide number of issues. According to Sowell:

One of the curious things about political opinions is how often the same people line up on opposite sides of different issues. The issues themselves may have no intrinsic connection with each other. They may range from military spending to drug laws to monetary policy to education. Yet the same familiar faces can be found glaring at each other from opposite sides of the political fence, again and again. It happens too often to be a coincidence and it is too uncontrolled to be a plot (Sowell, *Visions*, p. 3).

The *constrained vision* is primarily concerned with stability. This was the vision that dominated the earliest civilizations, including Egypt, Babylon, and ancient Israel. Novel ideas, new religions,[2] and individual contributions were considered suspect in hierarchical society. Indeed, authors in antiquity preferred to write pseudonymously rather than claim new ideas as their own; time-honored wisdom was far more likely to reach a readership.

For the constrained vision, law is what binds a society. Sigmund Freud argued that laws emerged to counter the instinctual, irrational, and pleasure-seeking actions of the individual (S. Freud, 1989). They served society by protecting lives and property. As Freud notes in *Totem and Taboo*:

> The law only forbids men to do what their instincts incline them to do; what nature itself prohibits and punishes, it would be superfluous for the law to prohibit and punish. Accordingly, we may always safely assume that crimes forbidden by law are crimes which many men have a natural propensity to commit (Freud, *Totem*, p. 204).

---

2   In the 1st CE, Judaism was accepted as an official religion and exempt from honoring the Roman gods. On the other hand, early Christians were persecuted for "atheism," as it was considered a "new" religion and therefore lacking in esteem. This would change in the 4th CE with Constantine's adoption of Christianity as the state religion.

The constrained vision recognizes the cyclical nature of time. As natural events tend to repeat, from the perspective of the constrained vision, so do human events. Whereas new technologies developed in antiquity, they did so far more slowly than today. On the other hand, the essential nature of man has changed little, if at all. The ancient Hebrew Book of Ecclesiastes 1:9 encapsulates this wisdom in the verse that, "There is nothing new under the sun."

By comparison, the *unconstrained* vision values the contributions of elite individuals above that of the collective. As Plato expressed in the *Republic*, governing was rightfully the domain of philosophers who were rational and intelligent and best suited to rule (Bloom, 2016). But Plato, too, was concerned with maintaining a stable society. He argued that democracy, in which all men, regardless of their capacities, have a say in governance, was a recipe for chaos and would ultimately require a tyrant to restore order. As Plato states in the *Republic:*

> The society (democracy) we have described can never grow into a reality or see the light of day, and there will be no end to the troubles of states, or indeed, my dear Glaucon, of humanity itself, till philosophers become rulers in this world, or till those we now call kings and rulers really and truly become philosophers, and political power and philosophy thus come into the same hands (Plato, *Republic*, p. 138, Author's parentheses).

But Plato viewed the physical world as an imperfect representation of supernal archetypes, viewing the latter as ontologically "real." Aristotle, unlike his teacher, Plato, was an empiricist whose primary focus was the physical world. Raphael's fresco of *The School of Athens* in the Vatican portrays Plato dressed in a blue toga with a finger pointing toward the sky, while Aristotle is dressed in red with his left palm facing the ground. This image exemplifies the conflict between the unconstrained vision of Plato and the constrained vision of Aristotle. The painting begs the question of whether the ideal and the real can be reconciled.

Law addresses man's imperfections. But for those holding the unconstrained vision, the perfectibility of man is a real possibility, if not now, then at some point in the future. For this reason, when deemed necessary by those holding the unconstrained vision, laws must yield to changing values.

Progressives in America today are heirs to the unconstrained vision.[3] They view the U.S. Constitution as a "living document" that can, and should, be changed via judicial interpretation to align with what they argue are evolving societal values. In contrast, Conservatives, guided by the constrained vision, argue that the fundamental tenets of the Constitution represent time-honored collective wisdom, and can only be changed by carefully considered legislation and affirmation of the electorate.

Conflicts between those holding the constrained and unconstrained visions have arisen in the past, primarily with respect to religious law and morality. Religious leaders have struggled with how to adopt the tenets of ancient laws and rituals prescribed in their founding documents to changing times, and these challenges have had immense influence on Western society. In many respects, as will be discussed, the culture wars are secularized versions of older religious conflicts, with opposing sides each claiming moral authority.

Those who hold to the unconstrained vision are wedded to the idea of linear time, in which time's arrow flows incessantly into the future.[4]

---

3   Throughout this text, the term liberal Progressive can be roughly equated with the Democratic Party, and Conservatives with the Republican Party. Although this is not entirely accurate, I think these terms best capture the mindset of those I am referring to, regardless of their party affiliation.

4   The monotheistic religions include a concept of the beginning and ending of time, so that there is a recognized progression. However, by adopting a calendar that is determined both by the sun and moon, Judaism maintains the notion of circular *chronos* that is not common to Christianity. Islam maintains a purely lunar calendar, and it is tempting to suggest that the absence of a solar contribution to the calendar has limited progress in the Islamic world.

As 6th BCE Greek philosopher Heraclitus argued, "No man steps into the *same* river twice;" rather, everything is constantly in flux. From this perspective, history can be seen as having limited relevance. The past may be viewed as having occurred within contexts that are no longer relevant in a changing world. Progress resists "outdated" modes of thought because those who are too young to remember the past are rarely concerned with it, unless they are *taught* to hold it in regard.

Progress can be difficult to evaluate. For those holding the unconstrained vision, change is invariably viewed as positive. As most of us today have been touched by the ideology of Progressivism by the educational process, what we accept as progress is rarely critically examined. However, it is dubious whether all change leads to improvement. When I was teaching at Harvard Medical School, every decade or so, a new dean would be appointed. Invariably, this resulted in major changes in the teaching curriculum. This is apparently how deans view their legacy. However, the rationale for their proposed changes was rarely clearly elucidated or critically examined; instead, it was sufficient to assume that change *must be* "progress."

HUMAN NATURE

Perceptions of human nature differ radically between those holding the two visions. The constrained vision holds that man is innately self-interested, prone to selfishness, and cannot be relied upon to respect the rights or the possessions of others unless legal constraints are in place. It recognizes "difference" as an inherent feature of the species, as some men are tall, others short; some ambitious, others, lazy, etc. Whereas the idea that all men share the same Creator is generally accepted, the gifts granted to them are not equal; indeed, genuine equality of men is considered nonsensical and *equity* misguided. This attitude corresponds to what French liberal philosopher Paul Ricouer pejoratively termed a "hermeneutic of suspicion," a term he applied to the views of Sigmund Freud, Karl Marx, and Frederick Nietzsche (Sims, 2003).

Freud ascribed human behavior to innate unconscious drives that are constrained by socialization. As social critic Phillip Rieff writes, "On the whole, Freud stands with Hobbes as opposed to Rousseau; not that man is good and society corrupts him, but that man is anarchic and society restrains him" (Rieff, 1979). But, as the results of efforts at achieving personal self-restraint are necessarily imperfect, man can be expected to continue to aggress against others when opportunities arise.

Freud's feelings about mankind were not complimentary:

> ...men are not gentle creatures, who want to be loved, and who at the most can defend themselves if attacked; they are, on the contrary, creatures among whose instinctual endowments is to be reckoned a powerful share of aggressiveness. As a result, their neighbor is for them not only a potential helper or sexual object, but also someone who tempts them to satisfy their aggressiveness on him, to exploit his capacity for work without compensation, to use him sexually without his consent, to seize his possessions, to humiliate him, to cause him pain, to torture and kill him. *Homo homini lupus* (Freud, *Civilization*, p. 58).

Anthropologists have noted that the moral veneer of a society quickly vanishes in reaction to war, disease, and famine. As I have noted elsewhere, morality is an evolved capacity of *homo sapiens* (R. Kradin, 1999), which can be lost when survival is threatened. Under conditions of threat and scarcity, few will continue to adhere to moral notions or display concern for their fellowman. From the perspective of the constrained vision, human nature is difficult to change, as there are inertial psychological and neurological forces that resist it (R.

L. Kradin, 2004). It follows that the possibility of perfecting human nature is an illusion, but one that stubbornly persists for those holding the unconstrained vision.

As Psalm 116:11 suggests, "All men are liars," an ancient idea recently confirmed by behavioral research. In the *Post-Truth Era*, psychologist Ralph Keyes argues that lying has in recent years become a widespread phenomenon in society (Keyes, 2016). The adage that, "Honesty is the best policy," apparently — as in the case of the young resident discussed above — no longer holds. Instead, "truth" has been replaced by the notion of "believability." Although the cause of the post-modern decline in truth-telling is complex, in part, it can be attributed to the decline of religious values in what is widely viewed as an increasingly immoral society.

WHAT IS GOOD?

Although Plato's notion of "the good" is one source of the unconstrained vision (Bloom, 2016), its notions of social justice have been adopted from the prophetic traditions of the Hebrew Bible, which were later eloquently espoused by Jesus. The Hebrew Bible admonishes man to show concern for the vulnerable in society. These groups were identified in Leviticus 23:22 as the widow, the orphan, the poor, and the "alien who dwells among you."[5] Accumulation of wealth and power were frowned upon. As Jesus taught in Mark 25, "It is easier for a camel to pass through the eye of a needle than for a rich man to enter the Kingdom of Heaven." Early Christian communities were socialist in nature, and they called for the redistribution and communal sharing of wealth. Acts describes dire consequences for those who refuse to

5   Several of the letters of Paul in the New Testament refer to the collection that he was accumulating to give to the poor in Jerusalem. The latter are assumed to be the Jewish Christian Ebionites (the poor) leaders of the nascent Church. Caring for the underprivileged is a feature of all religions but was greatly accentuated in the early Church.

share their wealth with the community. As New Testament scholar Bart Ehrman notes, "One of Jesus's characteristic teachings is that there will be a massive reversal of fortunes when the end time comes. Those who are rich and powerful now will be humbled then; those who are lowly and oppressed will be exalted" (Ehrman, 2012). These are ideas echoed by protesting Progressives on America's streets today.

But who is "disenfranchised" in America? Today, this is a matter of disagreement. Those holding the unconstrained vision argue that nothing truly belongs to the individual; instead, one's acquisitions are "gifts" to be shared with others. This is the secularized notion that, as all things come from God, they are to be shared by his creatures. This idea has been explicated both by Barack Obama and Elizabeth Warren. The left-wing Progressive senator from Massachusetts put it this way:

> There is nobody in this country who got rich on his own — nobody. You built a factory out there? Good for you. But I want to be clear. You moved your goods to market on the roads the rest of us paid for. You hired workers the rest of us paid to educate. You were safe in your factory because of police-forces and fire-forces that the rest of us paid for. You didn't have to worry that marauding bands would come and seize everything at your factory — and hire someone to protect against this — because of the work the rest of us did. Now look, you built a factory and it turned into something terrific, or a great idea. God bless — keep a big hunk of it. But part of the underlying social contract is, you take a hunk of that and pay forward for the next kid who comes along (Warren, CBS News, September 22, 2011).

In the past, Socialist ideas like this would not have gained traction with Americans. Instead, the entrepreneurial spirit of capitalism has reigned since the inception of the nation, and it has been responsible in large measure for America's exceptional standing in the world. This contrasts sharply with the Marxist experiments of the 20th CE in Russia and China, and recently in Venezuela, all of which proved disastrous in the eyes of most. While Democratic socialist countries in Europe have been modestly successful, they do not allow the entrepreneurial spirit that thrives in America. As social commentator David Horowitz notes (Horowitz, 2004):

> If socialism is not a viable system and capitalism is the only system that can produce wealth and freedom in a modern technological environment, what does this say about the revolutionary project? In the absence of a practical alternative, the revolutionary project is nihilism, the will to destroy without a concept of what to do next (Horowitz, *Unholy*, p. 58).

Furthermore, Americans are not inured to the needs of the poor and disadvantaged. America has adopted elements of socialism that benefit the poor, sick, and aged, including government-sponsored health care for the indigent (Medicaid) and Social Security for the aged. However, it is sadly the case that discrepancies in wealth have greatly increased in recent decades and the middle class that is key to the success of capitalism has been decreasing.

But while the aims of the unconstrained vision may be viewed as ethically commendable, they are also unrealistic. Utopian visions are, by their nature, both imaginal and futuristic. In the ancient world, they were linked to notions of an end time when, as the prophecy of Isaiah 11:6 states, "The wolf will live with the lamb, the leopard will lie down with the goat, the calf and the lion and the yearling together; and a little child will lead them." In the Messianic time, all will share equally and harmoniously. But that end time is always located somewhere in an unachievable future.

Eschatology, the study of this imagined end time, is a cardinal feature of the genre of apocalyptic literature. Apocalyptic ideas emerge in times of perceived hopelessness from sects that view themselves as disadvantaged and persecuted. They imagine a time when an aggrieved, but invariably morally superior elite, will be saved, while their enemies — by definition, anyone outside of the sect — will be damned and eliminated (Vermes, 2012). Among the monotheistic religions, Christianity is unique in having an apocalyptic text as part of its official canon, i.e., the book of *Revelation* — revelation being Latin for the Greek, apocalypse (*apokálypsis*).

This reflects Christianity's origin as an apocalyptic sect within Second Temple Judaism(s) (Cohen, 2014). As Albert Schweitzer noted in his *Search for the Historical Jesus*, the post-Easter Christians eagerly awaited the end of times when God would triumph over the minions of Satan, ushering in the "second coming" of Christ and the resurrection of the dead (Schweitzer, 1906). He argued that the historical Jesus was an apocalyptic seer who prophesized the imminent arrival of the Kingdom of God (Ehrman, 2012). All of the features of the apocalyptic genre can be identified in early Christian thought, including notions of radical duality of "good" versus "evil," divine revelation, salvation of the "select," and a final judgment at the end of times.

The dueling visions of secular America today are, in fact, expressions of the unconscious psychological motif that reimagines the ancient, and apparently perennial, conflict between forces of "light" and "darkness."[6] Despite their distaste for Christianity, the social justice positions of the Progressive left are reminiscent of Jesus's teachings. They focus on the redemption of modern historically aggrieved groups — blacks, women, and the LGBT community — and view

---

6 It is uncertain where this idea originated but it first appears in Judaism after the Babylonian exile. It is a core element of Persian Zoroastrianism and may have entered the consciousness of Judaism from there.

themselves as morally superior for championing their causes. The ideal future for these Progressives includes "cancelling" and "annihilating" Conservative voices that take issue with their agenda. Ultimately, they expect to usher in a new world order, the *Great Reset*, which is their secular version of the *Kingdom of God*.

IDEOLOGY

History has demonstrated that the unconstrained vision is generally the product of an intellectual elite and its followers, whom philosopher Hannah Arendt termed "the mob" (Arendt, 1976). Social transformation by elites is mediated by propaganda, intimidation, and the shaming of those judged to hold morally inferior values. In today's world, the aims of Progressives are being fostered by social media that disseminates information, and serves the role of "the mob" intent on "cancelling" its opponents.[7]

What has transpired over the last 60 years in America to account for this extreme political climate? During World War II and its aftermath, most Americans could accurately be described as patriotic and suspect of any movement that might encroach upon their freedom. In the 1950s, socialism was viewed as a serious threat by most Americans. But since the 1960s, Americans have increasingly embraced socialist ideas. Why, in the face of its known limitations, does it continue to carry appeal?

The answer must be sought in the *psychology* of those who espouse it. As Sowell suggests, the unconstrained vision is rooted in a strong desire for change and in idealized illusions, rather than in pragmatic realities. It is promoted by elite ideologues removed from the day-to-day concerns of the common man. Marx was a prime example. Born into a well-to-do family, he never held a consistent job, and was a

---

7   Indeed, within Judaism, it has been argued that it is not permitted to make efforts to speed the coming of the Messianic age.

notoriously poor husband and father. But he was an ideologue who imagined a class struggle between workers and their capitalist overseers that would result in a new utopian society. However, he recognized that America would not support his desire for revolution as no such class discrepancy existed here. Progressive Marxists in America also recognize this. For this reason, other historically aggrieved groups — women, blacks, LGTB groups — have been co-opted to take the place of the "working class." The "revolution" will be fought as a race war between whites and blacks, with the latter assisted by aggrieved women and those of heterogeneous gender.

The two-party system in America has, for a century, included the Democratic and Republican Parties, which currently align virtually isomorphically with the constrained and unconstrained visions, respectively. Whereas there are still centrist Republicans and Democrats — the latter referred to in the past as "liberals" — increasingly, the parties have assumed sharp differences on most subjects. Indeed, the parties have split along apocalyptic lines, with opposing views no longer tolerated. Instead, the opposition is seen and labeled as evil. In such an environment, compromise is useless; only complete victory, by legal or other means, over the "other" is possible. Indeed, Donald Trump was criticized for his lack of conciliatory tone with the left. But he recognized what many Americans still do not, which is that there is no reconciling with those who hate and seek to destroy you. For Progressives, the enemy is not limited to Donald Trump; it now includes *all* Americans who oppose their ideas.

AMERICAN RELIGION

As noted, the culture wars are essentially a religious conflict. Yet few perceive it as such. In *Americanism* (Gelernter, 2007), Yale scholar and polymath David Gelernter argues that:

> America is no secular republic; it's a biblical republic.
> Americanism is not a civic religion; it's a biblical religion...
> America is one of the most beautiful religious concepts man-
> kind has ever known. It's sublimely humane, built on strong
> evidence of humanity's ability to make life better (Gelernter,
> *Americanism*, p. 1).

Since its Puritan beginnings, America has been a Christian nation, and both the constrained and unconstrained visions found their roots in the Judeo-Christian ethic, but with distinct emphases on what represented the highest ethical good. Historically, Christianity is a syncretic merger of Jewish particularism and Hellenistic universalism. This melding leads necessarily to internal contradictions, which led the 2nd CE Church Father Tertullian to question what Hellenistic philosophy had in common with monotheistic faith. Most Americans continue to self-describe as Christians, but they tend to live lives that are secular except for occasional appearances at church. Yet one can still identify the Judeo-Christian ethic operating below the surface of the seemingly antithetical modes of morality in America.

The bicoastal urban areas of America are the strongholds of the Progressive movement. They are densely populated by academics, intellectuals, minorities, immigrants, and the entertainment and technology industries. These groups may claim to be Christian in some cases, but in fact they are best termed to believe in *Secular Humanism*, a largely atheistic philosophy that rejects religion as antithetical to reason. From this perspective, man is the ultimate source of progress and morality. On the other hand, much of middle America adheres to the constrained vision, and this includes America's agricultural heartland, the "Bible Belt," and relatively few ethnic minorities.

British philosophers, including John Locke and John Stuart Mill, whose works informed America's Founding Fathers, were enlightened men of their age, but they were also versed in the Bible (Gelernter, 2007; Huntington, 2005). The Founders, in turn, imagined America as a Christian nation, but rejected state-sponsored religion. Their concern was not that religion might interfere with American life; it was that a state religion could achieve hegemony over the political life of the nation, as was the case in England and mainland Europe. What today is widely considered the rightful "separation of Church and State" by Progressives is more extensive than the Founders intended or could possibly have imagined.

These men were pragmatists who worked together to achieve compromise between the constrained and unconstrained visions for the new nation (Ellis, 2015). However, they were near uniform in their recognition of the importance of Judeo-Christian morality for structuring American society. They attended to the prophetic warnings against the abuses of kings and recognized that power, if concentrated in the hands of a few, could be expected to lead to corruption and tyranny. Alexander Hamilton, James Madison and John Jay, who authored the *Federalist Papers*, were concerned with the selfish motives of men and the ability of power to corrupt when concentrated into the hands of even a well-intentioned few; after all, the new nation had recently fought a war to rid itself of the tyrannical actions of the English king. Hamilton was no democrat; he recognized the inequalities of men, as well as the importance of a central government ruled by an intellectual elite. For this reason, the new American nation was structured as a republic rather than an egalitarian democracy. As Hamilton noted in a speech in 1788 urging ratification of the new Constitution:

> It has been observed that a pure democracy if it were practicable would be the most perfect government. Experience has proved

that no position is more false than this. The ancient democracies in which the people themselves deliberated never possessed one good feature of government. Their very character was tyranny; their figure deformity (Hamilton, 1788, *Address to New York Delegation*).

To curb the accumulation of power, the Founders imposed a system of checks and balances on the new government, and a novel method of electing a president through an Electoral College that limited the influence of the more populated states. This system of government, based primarily on the constrained vision's assessment of the innate flaws in human nature, would prove successful for more than two centuries. But the experience in America would not be duplicated 13 years later in France, for reasons attributable to the opposing visions that formed the impetus for the two revolutions.

THE FRENCH REVOLUTION

The American Revolution began in 1776; the French Revolution began in 1789. Whereas both were rooted in Enlightenment ideas, the French experiment was an expression of the unconstrained vision, conceived primarily based on Rousseau's ideals of "liberty, equality, fraternity," and as a democracy that insisted upon the notion of man's perfectibility. Unlike the American experiment, the French revolt was a thoroughly secular enterprise, as the Catholic Church had been long allied with the power structure of the French aristocracy since the 8th CE (Schama, 1990). The French Revolution began with attacks on church corruption and on its clergy. The revolutionary authorities moved quickly to suppress the church, abolished the Catholic monarchy, nationalized church property, exiled 30,000 priests, and killed hundreds more (Holmes, 2016).

Mired in unfettered idealism, the Revolution quickly devolved into a *Reign of Terror*. As Kim Holmes suggests (Holmes, 2016):

> The Jacobins who followed Robespierre in establishing the Reign of Terror shared…a philosophy of "natural" republicanism; they believed that individuals who transgressed the laws of nature must be executed without judicial formalities. Anyone who stood against the republic stood against the people who were by right of their natural *goodness* above reproach. An enemy of the people became an enemy of the human race and thus guilty of treason (Holmes, *Closing*, p. 217-18).

As radical social reformer Saul Alinsky argued, revolutions must be extreme in their willingness to destroy what came before so that something "new" can emerge (Alinsky, 1971). Like the Jacobins, today's Progressives share this certitude concerning what they judge to be the absolute correctness of their moral "goodness."

The American Revolution was the product of a mercantile and agrarian society. American colonists were not downtrodden peasants and were accustomed to being treated like loyal and proper Englishmen. The American Revolution was carried out by a minority of colonists who resented being taxed and treated as "second class" citizens. The idea of "no taxation without representation," a popular protest among the colonists, was inconceivable in France, where representation for the peasantry was unknown. The colonists' concerns were vastly different than those who carried out the radical French experiment, the latter being psychologically motivated by envy and long-standing resentment. The French peasantry envied and hated its ruling class, as it had no possibility of ever sharing in its wealth or comforts. Envy is a strong motivating factor for hostility, but political action rooted in envy historically has demonstrated little long-term success. Instead, such movements archetypally begin with acts of destruction and soon devolve into anarchy, for they lack the reasoned underpinnings that ensure societal stability. Freud was aware of the role of envy in political revolts and recognized it as a source of instability (Rieff, 1979). As Phillip Rieff notes:

> By psychologizing social revolt and coercion, Freud weights his scale against impulse and in favor of law. Society is repressive; rebellion is not justified. For the freedom that humans seek is still the freedom to be master. The "conscious impulses" of rebellion have their unconscious sources in envy (Rieff, *Mind*, p. 227).

It is estimated that the French *Reign of Terror* resulted in as many as 40,000 deaths and ultimately required the dictatorship of Napoleon to restore order.

The French Revolution would become the template for all subsequent envy-based revolutions. Yet what should have been a singular bloody lesson in history was to be repeated again and again. Violent communist revolutions emerged in Russia in 1917 and China in 1950. Utopian in ideology, they were both rooted in envy, and resulted in large numbers of deaths. They also ultimately failed.

Yet the Progressive left will not admit that socialism is ill-conceived. Instead, they ignore history and continue to create new rationales for why these revolutions either had not actually failed or were not representative of "true" socialism. As a member of the socialist Green Party recently concluded, "There simply is no reason to examine the validity of socialism as a model. It is not socialism that was defeated in Eastern Europe and in the Soviet Union, because these systems were never socialist" (Horowitz, 2004, p. 58).

As political commentator Jonah Goldberg notes (Goldberg, 2009), the repugnance of Nazi racism causes Progressives to distance themselves from what they glibly term "fascism." But "socialism" was part of the moniker of "National Socialism" for a reason. In the 1930s, elements of German "National Socialism" elicited praise from American Progressives who admired its utopian vision. While it is commonplace today for Progressives to denigrate Conservatives as "fascists," or to vilify Mr. Trump as a "Nazi," it is Progressivism today that calls for the cooperation of corporations, with government based on the latter's self-anointed moral right to define and enact policies for the masses, even when they oppose established law. These are key elements of a totalitarian society.

Today, the new Biden administration is poised to undo the American system of checks and balances and the Bill of Rights, and to cooperate with corporations with the aim of instating a system of soft statist totalitarianism.

Progressivist Pedagogy

Progressivism has definite pedagogical aims, and it works hard at "instructing" the public. Sowell refers to these Progressive educators as "self-anointed" seers who believe that only they know what is best for America's future (Sowell, 2011). Barack Obama was a prime example of a Progressive pedagogue. Black, charismatic, articulate, and rigidly opinionated, Obama viewed himself as the embodied symbol of American progress. He enjoyed telling Americans what was best for them although, as Conservative commentator George Will noted, "Barack Obama has been the most loquacious president in American history, but can anyone remember anything that he said?" (Will, 2017)

Progressivism aims at indoctrinating the young into its ideology, and it has been far more successful than Conservatives have until now been willing to admit. Public schools and universities have been breeding grounds for new Progressives for decades. Young naïve students are "persuaded" through the themes of political correctness, racial diversity, and multiculturalism to pledge their allegiance to Progressive goals and to reject traditional American values. Since the 1960s, it has become increasingly unusual to hear a Conservative voice on today's college campuses, especially in the elite Ivy League. The degree of Progressive influence on young minds is both troubling and problematic, and conservative Americans need to address it soon if they are to reverse the path toward a one-party Progressive totalitarian state. President Trump's efforts at defunding federal aid to already well-endowed elite universities was an important first step at turning the tide of intolerant pedagogy.

Progressives in America correctly perceived themselves as threatened by Donald Trump's election. Trump represents all that they have been taught to reject for the future of America. He is neither politically correct nor afraid of expressing his displeasure. He is not fearful of feminist attacks on masculinity and refuses to be labeled as a "racist." He is not too cautious to make important decisions. Brash, self-promoting, wealthy, and ostentatious, if there was ever a man capable of inciting the repressed rage of a virtue-signaling obsessional, Trump *is* that man. On this, Progressives and "Never Trumpers" will agree wholeheartedly.

One of the cardinal rules of psychology is that when people become irrationally angered by the behavior of others, they are invariably reacting to a repressed aspect within themselves. Indeed, in treating obsessionals, one confronts deep-seated resistances to their own anger, grandiosity, racism, etc. These feelings and beliefs are repressed and split off from consciousness but invariably surface as projections. As Jungian analyst Marie-Louise von Franz noted (von Franz, 1985), projections require a "hook" and, for Progressives and virtuous "Never Trump" ideologues, Donald Trump is it.

As such, he is everything they despise about themselves but also envy. The intensity of their anger belies their degree of unconscious repression, and their reactions are paranoid and vindictive. In some cases, their reactions attain psychotic levels. Paranoid psychosis, as psychiatrists can attest, poses a real danger to others, as those suffering from it are capable of acting violently out of misperceived "self-defense." Ideologically rigid, narcissistically injured Progressives and "Never Trumpers" vowed to "resist" all actions by Trump's government. On a daily basis, they continued to seek new opportunities to impeach the president on fabricated charges and to "cancel" his supporters.

AN AVERSION TO TRUTH

Confrontations can be unpleasant and are best avoided when there is little at stake. But obsessionals exhibit a deep aversion to confronting uncomfortable truths. Such aversion is problematic when it results in their ignoring dire challenges that must be addressed. Many politicians, unlike Donald Trump, are obsessional personalities who are overly concerned with appearing "virtuous" and in having others approve of them. As a result, they often have no true convictions. With America witnessing daily protests, riots, and violence, many Democrats and Republicans continue to say and do nothing, preferring to stand idly by, paralyzed by their fear of confrontation. Enabling bad behavior by avoiding confrontation is a misguided approach that invariably fosters worse behaviors. But taking action in response to bad behavior assumes that one can discern right from wrong. That was relatively easy when society shared a common view of morality, but is no longer the case in America.

The Changing Psychological Milieu

Historian of psychiatry Edward Shorter has argued that human psychopathology is not fixed; rather, it is subject to prevailing cultural influences (Shorter, 1996). The classic example is the once-common disorder, *hysteria*. The symptoms of hysteria exhibited by patients in Freud's consulting room at the *fin de siècle* were flamboyant but triggered a search for an underlying physical disease. But now that we know a good deal more about the nervous system and psychosomatic disorders, these symptoms no longer convince physicians to seek a physical rather than a mental disorder (R. L. Kradin, 1997). On the other hand, hysteria remains relatively common in traditional societies that have not yet been suffused with scientific reasoning.

Obsessionality is also in flux. As religion historian Karen Armstrong suggests, there has been a progressive emphasis on cognitive processes in the West since the emergence of the *Age of Reason* (Armstrong, 2019). Intellectualization, control, and efficiency — the cardinal preoccupations of obsessional neurosis — are now increasingly prevalent in society. The focus on STEM curricula at the expense of the humanities fosters this one-sided approach to knowledge. Consider this statement of Progressive goals by Barack Obama on April 2013: "One of the things that I've been focused on as president is how we create an all-hands-on-deck approach to science, technology, engineering, and math.... We need to make this a priority to train an army of new teachers in these subject areas, and to make sure that all of us as a country are lifting up these subjects for the respect that they deserve."

In addition, e-mail, texting, and various social media platforms have people essentially "on-call" 24/7. It is now virtually impossible to avoid the incessant demands of the workplace, friends, and family. These pressures, coupled with the degradation of meaning in a postdeconstructionist and politically correct world, have resulted in heightened states of anxiety and repressed anger, both of which promote the obsessional style.

Digital technologies now allow institutions to monitor the activities of virtually anyone who is still "on the grid," which invites the control that obsessionals seek. But rather than recognize that their wish for control is driven by their existential anxiety, they instead rationalize it as an effort at maximizing efficiency, productivity, and safety. The obsessional focus on remaining safe through irrationally excessive efforts is what made the coronavirus epidemic a huge opportunity for the obsessionals of the Progressive left to exert control and limit the activities of their fellow Americans, especially in cities governed by Democratic Progressive mayors. It additionally allowed them to loosen the criteria for legal voting in the 2020 presidential election so that they could maintain that level of control over society.

The nexus of obsessional control with social justice issues has resulted in efforts at eradicating all dissenting voices in society by perceiving normal anger and criticism as evidence of hate, racism, and bigotry that must be expunged. But the virulent expressions of anger by obsessional Progressives expose the dishonesty of their approach. Skilled at creating rationales to support their actions, these "virtuous" and "kind" people see no contradiction in persecuting others relentlessly in vile ways. The true crime of Donald Trump and other Conservatives is simply that they dare disagree with the rigid perfectionistic aims of these obsessional neurotics.

Unfortunately, Progressive ideation is also at odds with evidence and common sense, with the latter being noticeably absent in this group. The diagnostic evidence of neurotic ideation is everywhere to be seen. Prioritizing the "rights" of illegal aliens, criminals, and domestic terrorists while ignoring the safety of America's citizenry defies common sense. The Biden administration's cutting jobs in the energy sector in the midst of an economic crisis created by the pandemic is nothing short of "stupid." Diversity and multiculturalism, among the highest priorities for Progressives today, benefit no one, and only serve to exacerbate divisive identity politics. Political correctness has evoked a great deal of anger from those who must suffer the nonsensical policies imposed by an insulated and neurotically obsessional elite. Psychologically speaking, this is a manifestation of the anger and self-defeating ideation that obsessional Progressives are projecting onto society.

The rationales that obsessionals unconsciously construct to guise their fear and anger are invariably riddled with irrationality and contradictions. I recently read a societal critique by a Progressive journalist. The book was well-written and engaging until the topic of Donald Trump arose. It then devolved into baseless *ad hominem* attacks: Trump was a "liar," a traitor," a "race baiter," an "anti-Semite." Obsessionals suffer from restricted affect and are generally out of touch with their emotions. When the latter surface, they are often inappropriate and excessive

Obsessionals have a propensity to repeat their mistakes. Freud termed this the *repetition compulsion*, and he attributed it to a failure to integrate repressed unconscious feelings into awareness so that conscious choice can take place. But the obsessional personality is structured on ideas that serve to defend against uncomfortable personal feelings. The new Biden administration's executive actions to raise taxes, cut jobs, and re-enter international treaties that were proven to hurt Americans are examples of a failure to learn from the errors of the past. When the few remaining Conservative media sites refer to Progressives resisting facts that do not fit their narrative, they correctly recognize that they are seeing obsessional defenses working at a collective level. Progressive ideology is a neurotic script that must be compulsively re-enacted in order to preserve a grandiose self-image guised as virtue and humility and to avoid having to accept previous historical failures.

The aim of studying history is not to memorize facts; rather, it is to improve one's ability to discern in order to make better choices in the future, but this is apparently lost on Progressives. Like the neurotic obsessional who is characteristically unwilling to accept help from others, these counter-dependent Progressives believe they can engineer their own fate and act as the architects of a new moral order.

HISTORY AND BELIEF

In the past, man recognized that he had a role in God's universe. But Progressives no longer believe that there is anything greater than themselves. Studies show that Progressives are less likely to hold traditional religious beliefs, and instead to view them as fanciful and anachronistic (C. Murray, 1984). The biblical tale of the Tower of Babel suggests that man's enthusiasm for "progress" may have limits, and that global unity, another popular Progressive notion, is naturally resisted by factors favoring family and nation. It is a truism that while the "many" strives to become "one," the "one" seeks to become "many." For the Abrahamic faiths, polytheistic religions that imagined the Godhead as the many avatars of nature was transformed into monotheistic belief. But paganism[8] is re-emerging as one of the many "isms" that attract modern man. Indeed, Progressive neurotic ambivalence is manifested by its simultaneous emphasis on globalism and "identity politics."

Witness England's recent rejection of the globalist European Union, and Trump's credo of "America First" as refutation of Barack Obama's globalist policies. Historically, large empires naturally tend

---

8   I am using the term "idolatry" metaphorically to refer to anything that is "worshipped" other than a supernal deity. It may be money, sex, or any "ism," including Progressivism.

to dissociate into nation states and these, in turn, into smaller ethnic communities, only to next re-assemble into larger confederations. The lesson is plain to see if one attends to the underlying psychology that drives history.

CHAPTER 1: VALUES AND NEUROSIS

"May you live in interesting times!"

— An ancient Chinese curse

The values of American society have been in flux since the 1960s. Change has led to strained relations between men and women, as well as enmity between those who hold religious beliefs and those who reject them. Feminism has transformed women's participation in the workplace, and easy access to contraception and abortion has freed women from the biological consequences of sexual activity. Identity politics have strained racial relations and currently threaten to rend the fabric of American society. Progressives today deny that great progress has transpired since the 1960s, but those who are older and honest enough can attest to it. Those who deny it are either too young to know better or frankly disingenuous.

GENDER IDENTITY

Today, bizarre notions of gender identity are challenging time-honored notions of biological difference. The role of biology as the primary determinant of sex has been questioned by those who, based on nothing beyond fantasy, prefer to believe that gender is exclusively psychologically "constructed." The extraordinary and troubling aspect of this illusion is that this idea is now shared by much of the scientific community, which is itself part of the obsessional Progressive establishment. The *American Academy of Pediatrics* in 2016 suggested that children as young as three years old *should* be encouraged to question their gender identity. However, psychiatrists who do not share Progressive ideas and who have treated transsexuals can attest that these individuals present a host of psychological issues unrelated to their gender choice. An article that appeared in the Daily Wire quoted Paul McHugh, the former chief of Psychiatry at Johns Hopkins, a prestigious medical institution (Prestigiacomo, 2016):

> Former Chief of Psychiatry at Johns Hopkins Hospital and Distinguished Service Professor of Psychiatry at Johns Hopkins University Dr. Paul R. McHugh blasted the Left's transgender movement, saying that those who enable the mental illness of transgenderism are "collaborating with madness."

Encouraging these individuals to identify as "stigmatized" is neither in their best interests nor those of society at large. The reaction from Progressives is that any challenge to this notion is evidence of bigotry. But that is not the case, and efforts to shame individuals who state facts should be firmly resisted.

Homosexuality is still condemned within traditional societies as an "abomination." In the heyday of psychoanalysis, which lasted through the 1960s, psychiatrists viewed homosexuality as an intractable neurosis with narcissistic underpinnings, i.e., as psychopathology. Today, Progressives insist that it is simply an alternative life style and one that should not only be accepted but publicly celebrated. Many applaud this as social progress, but others continue to harbor concerns that problems that often accompany the homosexual life style, including promiscuity, illicit drug use, and sexually transmitted diseases, are now largely left unaddressed.

A recent controversy concerning the demand of homosexual veterans to march as a separate group of "Out Vets" in the St. Patrick's Day parade in South Boston raises other societal concerns. The organizers of the event requested that they march with non-homosexual veterans as a sign of American veteran solidarity but they refused. The "Out Vets" were supported by Marty Walsh, the liberal Progressive mayor of Boston, and other legislators.[9] But the question of what does St. Patrick's Day, originally an Irish-Catholic observance, have in common with celebrating homosexuality remains unanswered, and the possible benefits of splitting Americans into ever-smaller factions each with their own agenda is not addressed. Personally, I don't value being "woke," but I do value being "conscious" and willing to ponder uncomfortable topics. This was once the standard of psychoanalytic inquiry, but today much of the psychotherapeutic community — Progressively oriented since its inception — has now been politicized by far-left narratives and is unwilling to examine the underside of the LGBT community.

RACISM

In America, despite tangible and steady advances in civil rights since the 1960s, accusations of racism, often baseless, have increased. The expectation that the first black American president would have promoted racial harmony proved incorrect. Instead, strident voices and violent elements within the black community insist that sufficient

9   Walsh, who imposed sweeping lockdowns during the recent pandemic, allowed mobs to tear down statues during the riots during the summer of 2020, and who has been implicated in corruption involving Boston labor unions, is apparently Joe Biden's choice for Secretary of Labor!

progress has not been made in civil rights and that "black lives matter," in their opinion, more than white lives. Using affirmative action programs as justification, people of color demand favored status with respect to admissions, accommodations, grading, and the structuring of curricula, and these are generally acceded to by college administrators. But as Conservative black author Shelby Steele notes, the current racial crisis is the result of a neurotic symbiosis between blacks who refuse to be responsible for their own future and obsessional whites who are plagued by neurotic guilt and highly uncomfortable with their "inner racist" (Steele, 2009).

Lest the lay reader think that this is simply "psychobabble," consider the following. Why would anyone who is *not* a racist be preoccupied with race, especially when there is *objective* evidence to support the idea that America may be one of the least racist nations? Why would anyone who is not a racist be disturbed by someone who makes that suggestion without any reason? Those who are comfortable with the knowledge that they are not racists would simply shrug it off as a groundless accusation. But that is not the case for many in America today. Instead, individuals, churches, and large corporations choose to signal their "virtue" by hanging "Black Lives Matters (BLM)" banners and signs on their lawns, and by donating large sums of money to what is, in truth, a domestic terrorist organization concerned with fostering criminal activities.

In an extraordinary display of both ignorance and neurotic self-hatred, Progressive whites have joined with militant blacks to denounce, in the most racist of terms, the very legitimacy of being white. One liberal professor noted that he didn't mind being called a "honkey" by blacks because "whites deserve it" (D'Souza, 1991). Some have gone as far as to suggest that being "white" is an innate, incurable pathology. Take, for example, the white male college professor who issued a statement that he was "dreaming of a white genocide for Christmas." Such outrageous ideas are taught and sanctioned by Progressive "scholars" on college campuses with impunity. Consider this response from the University of Wisconsin administration:

> A spokesman for the University of Wisconsin-Madison has shrugged off concerns over one of its students selling hoodies bearing the phrase "All White People Are Racist" in capital letters: "In this case, the individuals involved are exercising their rights to free speech and engaging in a private activity unrelated to their status as students," campus spokesman John Lucas said in an email to *The College Fix* (*The College Fix*, October 26, 2016).

First Amendment rights are granted to minorities on campuses, while comparable speech by whites is labeled "hate speech." This is antithetical to the very idea of free speech, which was once one of the great ideals of a liberal education in America. Today, even the hint of a criticism directed at "people of color" is virtually assured of triggering punitive action by an outraged "virtue-signaling" white administrator.

CRIME

A dangerous disregard for law has emerged in urban neighborhoods governed by Progressive Democrats. Consider the fact that literally thousands of blacks have died over the last ten years in the city of Chicago as the result of "black on black" crime:

> More than 750 people have been murdered in Chicago in 2016, the police said, a 58 percent increase over last year and the highest total since 1997. There have been more than 3,500 shootings in the city this year. Over Christmas weekend, at least 60

people were shot, 11 fatally, according to the Chicago Tribune (*Chicago Tribune*, Dec 28, 2016).

On Father's Day weekend 2020, more than 100 people were shot in Chicago, 14 fatally, including a 3-year-old boy. Violent crime has risen substantially in virtually every urban area over the last several years. These figures exceed the number of Americans killed in recent wars in the Middle East, and *far* exceed the number of blacks killed in the line of duty by white police officers (Mac Donald, 2016). Yet Progressive mayors, governors, and the mainstream press consistently ignore this grotesque situation because it does not conform with the Progressive narrative that only whites persecute blacks. If black lives *really* mattered to "Black Lives Matter" and their misguided white Progressive supporters, wouldn't they be concerned about this obscene loss of life in America? Hypocrisy? Maybe. But, perhaps more accurately, we are witnessing a collective obsessional neurosis inspired by Progressive propaganda that refuses to see what it does not want to see. The truth is that "Black Lives Matter" is a Marxist organization intent on stirring up racial hatred and transforming America. Their concern for "black lives" is a ruse to play on irrational white guilt. Those virtue-signaling whites who prefer to ignore this fact cannot be taken seriously when they claim that black lives matter, as *real* black lives apparently do not.

LOSS OF FREEDOM

Freedom of speech, guaranteed by the First Amendment to the U.S. Constitution, has been curtailed by the insidious aims of "political correctness" that limits individual speech based on imagined claims that it may cause discomfort to some. Some politically incorrect ideas are frankly too absurd to consider seriously, yet they have succeeded in becoming policy on university campuses and now have spread to

America's institutions at large. Accusations of "bigotry" and "racism" are routinely put forward to malign the reputations of innocent, decent people who dare to express opposing opinions, and who are given little opportunity for self-defense. Expressions of valid frustration are summarily labeled as "hate speech" and condemned. Progressive social media platforms routinely "cancel," i.e., remove messages that do not conform with their narrative.

Violent protests break out on college campuses when invited Conservative speakers dare to express views that differ with the Progressive agenda. A long list of accomplished Conservative scholars has been heckled off college campuses with angry epithets. William Bennett, a former secretary of Health, Education, and Welfare, stated in a July 28, 2016 television interview that he had not been invited to speak on an Ivy League college campus for decades. Political scientist Allan Bloom accurately characterized this as the "closing of the American mind" (Bloom, 2012):

> Every educational system has a moral goal that it tries to attain and that informs its curriculum. It wants to produce a certain kind of human being.... In some nations, the goal was the pious person, in others the warlike, in others the industrious. Always important is the political regime, which needs citizens who are in accord with its fundamental principles. Aristocracies want gentlemen, oligarchies men who respect and pursue money, and democracies lovers of equality. Democratic education, whether it admits it or not, wants and needs to produce men and women who have the tastes, knowledge, and character supportive of a democratic regime (Bloom, *Closing*, p. 26).

Unfortunately, what Bloom describes is no longer true in Progressive America.

ME TOO?

In a recent case at Columbia University — one repeated across American campuses — young male students accused of "rape" were expelled without recourse for defending themselves against what proved to be false allegations of misconduct by women.

> Even though Columbia found him not responsible for what had been alleged (rape), his suit claims the school was complicit in (his accuser's) long-running effort to destroy his reputation and declined to intervene because he is male. Some people believe the claim is absurd. Others say it's the wake-up call higher education needs to start protecting *all* students (Newsweek, December 18, 2015).

But perhaps the greatest travesty was the highly publicized nomination hearing of Justice Brett Kavanaugh for the U.S. Supreme Court. Kavanaugh — someone accurately described as a naïve "boy scout" — who was repeatedly accused, without evidence, of having engaged in sexual misconduct while in high school. Democrat senators at his confirmation hearings, supported by the mainstream media and Progressive protestors, insisted that the conservative judge was a sexual predator and unfit to serve as a justice on the High Court. Kavanaugh was repeatedly smeared, ridiculed, and forced to defend his innocence rather than being assumed to be innocent until compelling evidence to the contrary was brought forward.

The liberal American standard of jurisprudence, that individuals must be considered innocent until proven guilty, apparently no longer applies on Progressive college campuses, in corporations, or to Progressive legislators. This amounts to a serious and unacceptable undermining of American values.

NEWS

The primacy of perception over fact has resulted in a culture of fallacious ideas among so-called "journalists." The mainstream press currently unapologetically promotes its own biases and suppresses important news when it does not support the Progressive "narratives" to an extent not witnessed in recent times. Both the 2016 and 2020 U.S. presidential campaigns and their aftermaths have been plagued by biased news reporting to the extent that it is virtually impossible for readers and viewers to know when, or if, they are being told the truth. Instead, journalists have openly become Progressive activists, conducting an unrelenting concerted effort to denigrate and resist *all* the efforts of President Trump and his administration while hiding behind the First Amendment. The phenomenon of "fake news" has emerged in which journalists simply release news stories that have no factual basis or confirmed sources, justifying it as their defense of the moral superiority of the Progressive agenda. Journalists at the New York Times and Washington Post were awarded Pulitzer Prizes for their coverage of the "Russian Collusion" scandal that ultimately proved to have no basis in fact. As journalist Michael Chapman wrote in a blog entitled *Trump: Pulitzer Prizes on Russia "Collusion" Should Be Returned; They Were All Wrong* (Chapman, 2020):

> Given that the Justice Department has decided to drop the case against former National Security Adviser Lt. Gen. Michael Flynn and that the Office of National Intelligence has released formerly classified interviews revealing the FBI had no evidence of actual collusion between the Trump campaign and Russia, President Trump said the journalists who won Pulitzer Prizes for their "collusion" stories should return their prizes.

They won't return their prizes, nor will they retract their newspaper articles that falsely claimed "Russia Collusion." Accepting blame is not a consideration for the defended obsessional. Anyway, everyone *knows* that Trump must have stolen the election of 2016, because none of *our* friends voted for him. That's how America's Progressive journalists currently assess the truth.

The last 25 years have witnessed extraordinary technological progress with the advent of the Internet and other digital technologies. These new media sources have successfully encroached on traditional print and televised media. It is possible for virtually anyone to share observations and opinions on all manner of topics through social media. Unfortunately, few of these providers abide by the tenets of professional journalism.

Partisan journalism in America is not new. Indeed, only since the 20th CE have journalists been formally trained to be objective reporters of news, expected to verify their sources as legitimate. Certain media outlets such as the *New York Times* had acquired a reputation for high quality news reporting, but this was before digital media shortened the news cycle from several days to several minutes. Newspapers and television stations have been acquired by large Progressive-leaning corporate conglomerates that have their own globalist agendas, and journalists have been pressured to commercialize the news by making it both "politically correct" and "interesting," the latter generally inter-preted as controversial, scandalous, gory or, best of all, anti-Trump.

For those immersed in the world of the Internet and social media, these changes may seem a welcome democratization of ideas, but they raise serious concerns. Persistent "leaks" of classified government information and private conversations have put the reputations and safety of American citizens at risk.

Recently, the large Progressive digital and social media corporations have cooperated to suppress news by deplatforming Donald Trump, any number of Conservative voices, and their social media competition (*Parler*), with no *real* justification. This level of censorship is both unprecedented and dangerous, but it is symptomatic of the conflation of obsessional and grandiose impulses exhibited by today's Progressive elites.

THE OBSESSIONAL NARCISSIST

Social psychology applies the tenets of individual psychology to the behaviors of society. In the 1970s, cultural historian Christopher Lasch offered a poignant argument that America had become a culture of narcissism (Lasch, 1979) in which self-interest, entitlement, and instant gratification had outstripped traditional concerns for others. The notion of hard work leading to the accumulation of wealth over a lifetime was challenged by "20-somethings" who have become fabulously wealthy overnight through financial speculation or by innovating technologies.

This trend toward narcissism has been accompanied by levels of psychological rigidity that are properly characterized as *obsessional*. The manifestations of this obsessional trend appear to be the result of converging factors in the culture including 1) increased existential insecurity, 2) declining moral values, 3) digital technologies that can relay information instantaneously and uncensored, 4) social media that promotes the uncritical sharing of ideas, or "groupthink" at the expense of individual autonomy, and 5) the effects of feminism and identity politics.

AN UNCONSCIOUS SOCIETY

Perhaps Sigmund Freud's greatest contribution to the world of ideas was recognition that behaviors are determined by motives beyond consciousness, what he termed unconscious drives (*trieb*). Freud was interested in how society participated in the repression of ideas and feelings, and viewed himself as a reformer intent on freeing individuals from the prevailing sexual repression of the Victorian age. He argued, in *Civilization and its Discontents*, that the unconscious drives of the individual invariably conflict with the civilizing goals of society (S. Freud, 1930). Socialization requires parents and educators to impose reasonable restraints on the instinctual desires of the child. The dilemma for society is how to achieve an optimal balance between instinct and restraint. Freud imagined a society in which individual instincts were not overly repressed and prone to neurosis, but one that also preserved societal stability. Extremes of strictness or permissiveness were likely to defeat the goal. As he suggested:

> Man is fundamentally antisocial. Society must domesticate him, must allow some satisfaction of biological — and hence ineradicable — drives; but for the most part society must refine and adroitly check man's basic impulses. In consequence of this suppression of natural impulses by society something miraculous happens: the suppressed drives turn into strivings that are culturally valuable and thus become the human basis for culture (Freud, *Civilization*, p. 8).

This summarizes Freud's notion of *sublimation* by which the instinctual impulses of the individual are transformed into societally acceptable and creative activities.

In his early theory of mind, Freud suggested that the primary unconscious drive was a sexual one, aimed at pleasure and procreation. As Sulloway concludes in *Freud: Biologist of the Mind*, like other scientists of his time, Freud was influenced by Darwin's competitive vision of survival of the fittest (Sulloway, 1979). Freud viewed sex as the primal drive that served the adaptive aims of evolution. But, by 1920, in response to the traumatic events of the Great War, and masochistic behaviors that he was observing in analysis, he concluded that aggression was a second separate innate human drive (S. Freud, 1923).

Today, few modern psychoanalytical theorists are classical Freudians. Most have broadened their understanding of unconscious motivations to include affiliative behavior as an inborn primary determinant of human activity. Successful attachment to early caretakers is a universal feature of infancy required for survival (Bowlby, 1969). Unfortunately, attachments are also subject to post-natal distortions that result from repeated microtraumas or gross abuses in caretaking. Theorists have argued that a variety of anxiety-driven attachment styles are causally associated with adult psychopathologies. Wiltgen, et al., have demonstrated that insecure and avoidant attachment styles predict the appearance of adult rigid obsessional personality traits (Wiltgen, et al., 2015).

Correlations between attachment anxiety/avoidance with specific obsessional personality disorder diagnostic criteria revealed that attachment avoidance was correlated with four of eight obsessional personality disorder criteria across the full sample. Within the subset of obsessional personality disorder patients, attachment avoidance was significantly correlated with obsessional personality disorder criterion excessively devoted to work and productivity to the exclusion of leisure activities and friendship (Wittgen, et al., p. 412).

As a consequence, avoidance is the primary relational strategy of the obsessional. It is, as will be discussed, also the underlying psychological motivation for "political correctness," which now characterizes obsessional society.

An explanatory model of social psychology must account for the forces that promote and disrupt interpersonal affiliation, and include consideration of motives unknown to the individual and by extension to the group. As psychoanalyst Erich Fromm contended, a social psychology that ignores unconscious factors risks missing critical underlying truths operating in society (Fromm, 1960). Unfortunately, as these are not expressed directly, only with experience is it possible to surmise what is driving overt behavior.

PROJECTION

Freud argued that all behaviors are multi-determinate. It is impossible to accurately attribute the cause of behavior to a single motive; instead, a variety are invariably at play. Jung argued that the greatest problem facing modern man was an inability to assume responsibility for his unconscious motivations because, without recognizing their true inner source, they were prone to being *projected* onto others. As Jung wrote:

> Just as we tend to assume that the world is as we see it, we naïvely suppose that people are as we imagine them to be.... All the contents of our unconscious are constantly being projected into our surroundings, and it is only by recognizing certain properties of the objects as projections, or *imagos,* that we are able to distinguish them from the real properties of the objects.... *Cum grano salis,* we always see our own unavowed mistakes in our opponent. Excellent examples of this are to be found in all personal quarrels. Unless we are possessed of an unusual degree of self-awareness, we shall never see through our projections but must always succumb to them, because the mind in its natural state presupposes the existence of such

projections. It is the natural and given thing for unconscious contents to be projected (Jung, *General Aspects of Dream Psychology*, par. 507).

Jung provides a detailed explanation of projection as a mental process, an unconscious dialogue with both participants sharing in its construction, albeit to varying degrees. Projections are not simply a psychological mode of purging unacceptable intrapsychic contents; they are also integral to the assessment and integration of experiences, as they are evoked by what is unknown about the "other." Like nature, the human psyche abhors a vacuum, and it naturally tends to project known experience onto people, things, and situations that are inadequately or completely unknown. One sees this type of behavior in the parents of infants and pet owners who imagine that they know what they are "thinking" or "feeling" (R. Kradin, 2007):

In psychoanalytic thought, projection reflects a defense of the ego in which mental contents are unconsciously transferred onto others. Personality styles that include rigidly defended ego states are characterized by excessive reliance on projection. Freud referred to the patient's projections onto the analyst as transference and recognized that the abstinence of the analyst tended to promote transference projections. Jung recognized that projection is an archetypal psychological activity that is activated by insufficient knowledge of one's environment, including others (Kradin, *Minding*, p. 1).

In this regard, the experiences of those within our culture have become so divided and encapsulated that it is virtually impossible for them to know anything about the other. As a consequence, this knowledge vacuum is filled by projections. To the Progressive left, their

Conservative countrymen live in the "boondocks" and are ignorant "gun-toting" religious fanatics. Conservatives, on the other hand, may see Progressives as immoral city dwellers who prefer Chardonnay to a beer.

Kleinian psychoanalyst Thomas Ogden has suggested that mentalization, i.e., the ability to formulate thought, develops from a dynamic of interpersonal projection that is subsequently re-collected by the source of the projection in the service of realizing greater objectivity (Ogden, 2005). In rigid psychopathologies, such as obsessionality, the re-collection of projections is defective, and this results in a persistent distortion of reality. The extensive projections on the part of Progressives onto President Trump, as well as resistance to accept realities that do not accord with their preconceived ideology, is symptomatic of obsessional rigidity and resistance to seeing the world clearly. It results in an intractable difficulty in learning from experience or from anyone who is not like-minded. It is akin to what psychoanalyst Melanie Klein termed a paranoid position (Klein, 1958) typical of the obsessional.

The elements most prone to projection are thoughts and feelings that are disavowed by ego-consciousness and whose emergence is signaled by anxiety. In reaction to this "signal anxiety," unacceptable ideas and feelings are automatically and rapidly "purged" before being consciously realized. This is achieved by misattributing them to others. Jung referred to these disavowed aspects of psyche as "shadow." A literary example of the "shadow" was offered by J.M. Barrie in *Peter Pan in Kensington Gardens*. Peter, a *puer aeturnus*, is resistant to confronting the unpleasantries that adults must come to grips with as part of the disillusionment of growing up. He refuses to do so and although his "adopted mother," Wendy, attempts to sew Peter's shadow back on, she is unsuccessful (Barrie, 1906).

Progressives perceive a "hook" for their projections in President

Trump, but the true source of their disdain is *within* them. Consider the innumerable projections of Progressive Democrats: Trump will not accept the results of the 2020 election if he loses (fairly); Trump is colluding with Russia (all evidence indicates that it was the Clinton campaign that was); Trump is a racist (Joe Biden: "Poor kids are as bright as white kids"); Trump separates mothers from children at the border (a standard technique under the Obama administration), and the list goes on.

Obsessionals are perfectionistic and critical. They fear their own anger; they hate themselves and others, and make concerted efforts to guise it with socially acceptable politeness. Freud recognized that obsessional neurosis as the result of an overly controlled upbringing, i.e., over-socialization. The skills of many politicians are based on carefully guising public displays of anger. They worry about revealing their contempt of others and constantly seek self-affirmation. They are careful not to offend anyone who might potentially vote for them, an obsessional style that severely limits the ability to have any real convictions. And this is true on both sides of the aisle. Political correctness is the obsessional's dream. Trump's spontaneity and unpredictability produce substantial anxiety for obsessionals who must constantly suppress their own chaotic feelings.

Due to their hypersensitivity to the criticism, Progressives are unable to accept responsibility for their actions. Months after her defeat, Secretary Clinton and her Progressive supporters remained intent on attributing their ill-conceived campaign on external factors, blaming their defeat on outside "interference by Russia," the press, the FBI director, computer hackers, etc., rather than accepting the fact that she was a singularly unlikable candidate. Instead, they have spent the last four years intent on undoing reality, a characteristic obsessional defense mechanism. In the 2020 presidential election, campaign strategists wisely chose to keep Joe Biden out of sight so he could not answer any questions about his intended policies or past behaviors. With the assistance of a singularly uncurious media, the strategy worked.

Although Progressives may be correct concerning the truth of "unconscious racism," neither they nor anyone else is, or ever will be, immune to it. The accusation denies the normal innate activities of the human mind. Modern neuroscience confirms that we all experience *automatic* subliminal evaluations of others. It is the normal role of the brain to scan the environment to identify change and difference in its environment. Studies show that the brain's subcortical structures, including the amygdala and anterior cingulate gyrus, are actively engaged in identifying environmental situations, persons, things, and places that potentially represent danger. As Robert Sapolsky notes in *Behavior: The Biology of Human Behavior at its Best and Worst*, "The amygdala helps to mediate both innate and learned fear…the amygdala injects implicit fear and distrust into social decision making"(Sapolsky, 2017).

These rapid "reflex" evaluations are subsequently re-evaluated by slower neural pathways within the left frontal cortex that allow for rational determinations concerning the degree of danger. Anyone with any common sense can be expected to react fearfully to a group of young blacks wearing "hoodies" on an urban street at night. Indeed, to not do so might be to potentially place oneself in harm's way. This is neither "bigotry" nor "racism;" it is a learned response based on knowledge of real crime rates in urban cities, and the fact that most violent urban crimes are committed by young men of color. That is a *fact*; to deny it is to be either naïve or disingenuous. Certainly, it is not healthy to feel guilty about it. Facts matter; human biology is what it is, as are crime statistics for urban America, whether one likes them or not. We are free to tell ourselves whatever we choose but, when we negate reality, that is neurotic or worse.

Having established this, it follows that *no one* deserves to be criticized for their human nature. One cannot be held responsible for *feelings* unless they are consciously acted upon to limit the freedom of others. The legal system recognizes this truth; at least it used to. The expectation of a world without bias is naïve, perfectionistic, and a fantasy. It assumes a level of moral purity on the part of those leveling such criticisms that they do not — and never will — possess.[10] Efforts at singling out whites, as has recently occurred in the City of Seattle for training about the evils of "white privilege," should be federally prosecuted for the "racist hate crime" that it is. Instead, the Progressive Biden administration is mandating "racial sensitivity" training for government workers.

Progressives must be made to recognize that, when they casually label others "racists" or "bigots," their behavior differs little from that of the Nazis who demonized Jews or the Southern racists who persecuted blacks. The underlying psychology of the vitriolic devaluation of Donald Trump, his supporters, or of white men on college campuses is genuine bigotry. That is the *truth* Progressives choose to deny.

Therapists who have treated couples know that projections are the cause of the constant bickering that one observes in troubled marriages, and that often lead to divorce. The last time Americans went through a "divorce" was the Civil War. It, too, was triggered by the election of an enormously unpopular president, Abraham Lincoln.

10 A colleague of mine recently told me that a relative who lives in Southern California is an administrator of a newly constructed hospital in San Diego. She told him the new complex had been built in a northern suburb of the city to reduce the number of illegal immigrants giving birth there. At the same time, the community encourages "open borders." It is difficult to know how to explain such decisions other than as hypocritical.

WHOSE REALITY?

Jungian psychoanalyst Maria von Franz observed (von Franz, 1985) that the accuracy of projections is ultimately determined by consensus. In this vein, author Gary Zukav argues (Zukav, 2012):

> "Reality" is what we take to be true. What we take to be true is what we believe. What we believe is based upon our perceptions. What we perceive depends upon what we look for. What we look for depends upon what we think. What we think depends upon what we perceive. What we perceive determines what we believe. What we believe determines what we take to be true. What we take to be true is our reality (Zukav, *Dancing*, p. 310).

In the past, most Americans agreed upon the essential "good" of America as a nation; they showed respect for authority and treasured impartial justice. But, in today's America, essentially evenly divided concerning perceptions of what is "good," how is "reality" to determined?

Social scientist Peter Berger, whose text, the *Social Construction of Reality,* became the source of much of the relativism that characterizes modern academic thought, registered his own objections to the interpretation of his work by left-leaning scholars (Berger & Luckmann, 1966):

> Our concept of the social construction of reality in no way implies that there are no facts. Of course, there are physical facts to be determined empirically from the fact that a massacre took place to the fact that someone stole my car. But the very concept of objectivation implies that there are social facts as well, with a robust reality that can be discovered regardless of our wishes...but the various narratives...correspond very

neatly with a definition of schizophrenia, when one can no longer distinguish between reality and one's fantasies (Berger and Luckman, *Social*, p. 133).

Unfortunately, we live in a society that is exhibiting an increasing propensity to create "realities" that have little basis in fact. What Berger describes as "schizophrenia" is more properly termed neurotic illusion, although frankly delusional ideation is also evident as "Trump Derangement Syndrome."

A comparable mode of perception was described as *animus* opinions by Emma Jung. In *Anima and Animus*, she described women "with fixed ideas, collective opinions and unconscious *a priori* assumptions that lay claim to absolute truth. In a woman who is identified with the animus (called animus-possession), Eros generally takes second place to Logos (E. Jung, 1985).

Unpacking the Jungian jargon, this means that, for uncertain psychological reasons, some women tend to have strong ideas that are based on their feelings rather than logic. This mode of perception has become widespread in society today and is currently expressed by both men and women. Rational thinking on social issues based on objective facts appears to be receding in modern American society. The level of permissiveness seen in America maps directly with the imposition of feminist thought on society. Female modes of relational thinking may help explain current objections to borders, the resistance to punitive actions by the criminal justice system, acceptance of the LGBT community, intolerance toward recognizing real racial differences, and much of the anger concerning Trump's masculine persona.

DEFINING NEUROSIS

According to psychoanalyst David Shapiro in *Autonomy and Rigid Character* (Shapiro, 1981):

> Neurosis in one way or another restricts subjective experience. Neurotic attitudes and ways of thinking having developed in shrinking or self-protective reaction to conflict or discomfort, then tend to inhibit the full conscious experience of conflictual and discomforting feelings or motivations. This is not merely the conscious experience of particular memories, feelings, or wishes that are inhibited, but whole classes of subjective experience that are inimical to these attitudes are also inhibited (Shapiro, *Autonomy*, p. 54).

But to diagnose neurosis, which is the expression of an "unhealthy" mind, one must first define mental health, which is not an easy task. The concept of psychopathology evokes criticism by Progressive psychotherapists, who view it as "stigmatizing." Although there are classifications of personality that are primarily descriptive, it is virtually impossible to identify one that is devoid of implied pathology. Indeed, it is impossible to develop a metapsychology for therapeutics that is not value-laden. The term "therapy" in Greek literally means "healing," and therefore implies a condition that requires treatment.

Rieff suggests in *Triumph of the Therapeutic* that large sectors of society today, influenced by Freudian psychology, view themselves as in need of therapy. This preponderance of therapeutics undermines the notion of health and a role for personal responsibility (Rieff, 1966). After all, what can health mean if virtually everyone is "sick?" The notion that "It's not your fault," is frequently heard today, and it creates a condition in which many Americans no longer have the motivation to help themselves, and instead consider themselves victims of a dysfunctional childhood and society.

Physical health is operationally defined by adaptive plasticity of the physiological activities of the body. A variety of homeostatic mechanisms function to maintain bodily functions within defined limits, e.g., body temperature, blood sugar levels, etc. Health may be modeled mathematically as *deterministic chaos,* in which physiological systems respond adaptively to environmental perturbations while maintaining strict boundaries (R. Kradin, 2008). From this perspective, disease may be defined as a rigid non-adaptive response to perturbation. If one adopts a comparable definition for mental health, then neurosis is a limited range of responses to a changing environment, much as Shapiro defined it as "restricted experience" (Shapiro, 1981). Indeed, psychologists regularly refer to "rigid personalities" and recognize the pattern among neurotics compulsively to repeat behaviors that are self-defeating.

Psychoanalyst Erich Fromm noted that mental health and the aims of a society are not necessarily the same (Fromm, 1960):

The person who is healthy in terms of being well-adapted is often less healthy than the neurotic person in terms of human values. Often, the latter is well adapted only at the expense of having given up his self in order to become more or less the person he believes he is expected to be. All genuine individuality and spontaneity may have been lost…the neurotic person can be characterized as somebody who was not successful and instead of expressing his self productively, he sought salvation through neurotic symptoms and by withdrawing into phantasy life. Nevertheless, from the standpoint of human values, he is less crippled than the kind of normal person who has lost his individuality altogether (Fromm, *Escape*, p. 138).

Society tends to reward certain neurotic styles. For example, obsessionals are often intelligent and hard-working. Pressure may be exerted on individuals from an early age to conform through systems of reward and punishment that target ideas, speech, and actions in directions that favor obsessionality. The success of such a society is measured by conformity, but genuine autonomy is repressed. Those who do not conform are then labeled wrong-minded by society, although their degree of genuine autonomy may, in fact, be better developed. In today's politically correct society, real mental health is punished while obsessional conformity is rewarded. This was the situation in the Victorian era that Freud was addressing. Times have changed, but the increasing obsessional traits in today's society may call for a different societal approach.[11]

The ability to maintain a neurosis requires persistent perceptual and interpretive distortions. When these are extreme and inflexible, they can reach the level of delusion, which is the psychiatric definition of psychosis. The boundaries between neurosis and psychosis are permeable and, under conditions of stress, neurotic illusions can devolve into psychotic delusions, often of a paranoid type. Trump's election in 2016 is an example of such stress, and it has led to four years of collective societal psychosis.

According to Jung, neurosis results from a one-sided imbalance in the functional capacities of the psyche. Furthermore, individuals with different one-sided personality types will experience difficulties understanding each other due to different perceptions and interpretations of their sensory experience. Consequently, they may disagree as

---

11 I address this issue in *Breakdown: How Progressive Ideology is Eroding Morality and Redefining Mental Health in America* (2020, Defiance Press).

to what constitutes "reality" and what represents the highest "good" for a society.

> Only a limited number of contents can be held in the conscious field at the same time, and of these only a few can attain the highest grade of consciousness. The activity of consciousness is selective. Selection demands direction. But direction requires the exclusion of everything irrelevant. This is bound to make the conscious orientation one-sided. The contents that are excluded and inhibited by the chosen direction sink into the unconscious, where they form a counterweight to the conscious orientation (Jung, *Psychological Types,* par. 694).

The obsessional shows a propensity for thinking and can be expected to differ in his assessments of reality from those who lead with their feelings. When a society becomes polarized around different psychological types, dialogue may prove impossible. When this occurs within a marriage, it often leads to divorce. But what is the recourse when a country is subject to extreme typological polarization?

Chapter 2: The Obsessional Personality

Two roads diverged in a yellow wood,
and sorry that I could not travel both,
and be one traveler, long I stood.
— Robert Frost, *The Road Not Taken*

To gain a deeper appreciation of what it means to be obsessional, it is helpful to explicate the range of thoughts and behaviors that obsessionals tend to exhibit. Compulsiveness is the behavioral counterpart of obsessionality. It is widely understood as a mode of relieving anxiety and countering the lack of joy, i.e., *anhedonia*, that accompanies obsessionality (R. L. Kradin, 2004).[12] These compulsions manifest as *excessive* work, cleaning, exercise, sexuality, and drug and other addictions. Most normal people share some of these features but when they are extreme, they represent an obsessional neurosis.

Obsessionality appears to occur along what may be a spectrum ranging from obsessional style, to obsessional personality disorder (OPD), to severe obsessive-compulsive disorder (OCD) (Association,

---

12 One of the complaints heard in society today by comedians is the inability of young Progressives on college campuses to laugh. What was once viewed as funny is now seen as politically incorrect by this grim group.

1994). It is impossible to assess the actual frequency of obsessional personalities in society, as few seek psychiatric care and thereby elude accounting. However, there are large numbers of individuals with obsessional styles in society, and empirical observation suggests that their numbers are increasing.

Many obsessionals accept the label with pride. They view their neurotic quest for perfection as meritorious, and rationalize away their ritualistic behaviors as benign idiosyncrasies. The impact of obsessionals on society is substantial, as they often attain positions of authority and power. They may excel at the workplace due to hard work and attention to detail. When they come to clinical attention, it is generally because their levels of perfectionism or critical remarks have disturbed co-workers or undermined domestic relationships. Their restricted feeling and work ethic can produce an aura of sterility and a preoccupation with picayune rules. Their concept of "progress" tends to be focused on procedural efficiency rather than new content. Indeed, few Progressive Democrats produce new ideas; instead, they are wed to notions of higher taxes and more governmental controls that have proved unsuccessful in the past. They lack the "vision thing."

Jung referred to obsessionals as extraverted "thinking-sensation" types, emphasizing what he viewed as their dominant psychological functions (C.G. Jung, 1972). Obsessionals are empirically recognized to exhibit restricted "feeling" and limited "intuition." While Jung's typology is accurate, it does not address the full range of behaviors that one encounters in obsessionals, nor does it provide potential causal explanations for this personality style.

Obsessional neurosis holds a privileged place in the history of psychopathology. Along with "hysteria," it was one of the two major neurotic styles to be recognized prior to the advent of psychoanalysis. As Shapiro notes (Shapiro, 1981):

Two neurotic modes of volitional action — that of hysterical and impulsive characters and certain passive "weak" individuals, and that of rigid character — serve to illustrate the forms of conscious self-direction. Among the former, aims are exceedingly vague and intentions are hardly articulated or self-conscious. Such a person may feel that he has no aims of his own, that his actions are entirely determined by force of circumstance or the expectations of others.... Among rigid characters, on the other hand, there is an extraordinary degree of articulation and self-consciousness of aim and purpose, an often excruciating consciousness of choice and decision, and great deliberateness of action (Shapiro, *Autonomy*, p. 18).

The hysterical style was more often observed in women, whereas obsessionality was considered a masculine personality style in the past, when gender differences were clearer and accepted as possible.

The factors that contribute to the psychogenesis of obsessionality are uncertain, but genetics, developmental and sexual traumas, and cultural values likely all contribute (*Diagnostic and Statistical Manual of Mental Disorders-V*, 2010). The *Diagnostic Statistical Manual (DSM)-IV* included obsessive-compulsive disorder (OCD) as an anxiety disorder, emphasizing the cardinal role that anxiety plays in its symptomatology. Indeed, phobias and generalized anxiety are common co-morbidities in those with obsessional styles. However, the most recent nosology of psychopathology has removed OCD from the Axis I affect disorders, while continuing to characterize it as distinct from the more common and less disabling obsessional personality disorder (OPD). Nevertheless, the symptoms and behaviors of those with OCD and OPD exhibit substantial overlap.

As Shapiro notes, obsessional personality is part of a psychodynamic spectrum of "rigid personality disorders" that includes obsessional, narcissistic, and paranoid features (Shapiro, 1981). It can be difficult in practice to distinguish them with accuracy. What they share from a psychodynamic perspective is a largely impermeable barrier between ego-consciousness and subliminal disavowed thoughts and feelings. These individuals are hypersensitive to criticism, show difficulties in regulating self-esteem, and are prone to projective defenses that exteriorize disavowed "flaws" onto others, rather than taking responsibility for them (Salzman, 1977).

Freud noted early in his career as a psychoanalyst that the obsessional shares features with the young child who insists on perfection, and displays "magical thinking" aimed at securing themselves from danger via omnipotence of thought. Obsessionality tends to crystalize in adolescence and then persists throughout the lifespan. In his theorizing on obsessional neurosis in the *Rat Man* and *Notes Upon a Case of Obsessional Neurosis* (1909), Freud suggested that conflicted feelings of love and hate for early caretakers were the major source of obsessional ambivalence, doubt, and compulsion. In *Inhibitions, Symptoms and Anxiety* (S. Freud, 1959), he described the two main defense mechanisms of obsessional neurosis as the *avoidance of affect* and the *undoing of actions*.

The rigid boundary between conscious and unconscious elements is recapitulated in the obsessional's relationships with others. He may be exceedingly polite but also reserved and "cool." He maintains intellectual defenses to ward others off, and tends to avoid commitments and intimacy. Obsessionals have perfectionistic standards, are inclined to be ideologues, and will cling rigidly to their beliefs, even in the face of contradictory evidence.

ANXIETY

Obsessionals report anxiety as a background affect. They are easily overwhelmed by environmental stressors and perceived chaos or strong feelings. The obsessional responds to anxiety with compulsive activities that transiently mask it, but it soon returns once these activities cease. The source of anxiety is generally ill-perceived. Some report "free-floating anxiety," i.e., with no obvious source, whereas others report specific phobias. Often, both co-exist. When psychoanalyzed in depth, these anxieties can be mapped to fears of being overwhelmed, maintaining boundaries, physical injury, mental dissolution, and ultimately to a fear of death (Salzman, 1977).

The current crisis concerning the coronavirus and the wearing of masks is a typical obsessional motif. Unable in some cases to accept even minimal risk, the obsessional Progressive rationalizes shutting down the economy and schools, potentially forever, to reduce their anxieties. Unfortunately, their solutions are not based on facts. While there are genuine risks in the midst of a pandemic, no one need fear catching the virus while riding a bicycle outdoors or when they are distanced from others. Children are not at high risk of becoming ill or even of transmitting the virus. This is what the current evidence shows.

The politicization of wearing masks is ultimately a struggle between obsessionals and those who do not share their level of concern. Trump angers the Progressive left because he shames them for being cowards, which they are. But when there is a local outbreak of the virus, or if a rare child succumbs to it, they will see this as righteous confirmation of their concerns.

Obsessionals adopt cognitive strategies to restrain their anger. These thought-promoting strategies are part of the socialization project of childhood. Obsessionals, as Fromm suggests, are overly socialized and covertly resentful of being so (Fromm, 1960). They exhibit an affinity for "rational" thought and are careful in the construction of their speech. While they may be highly intelligent, their rationales are subliminally deceptive and primarily serve to obscure their fears. The extremity of their concerns is beyond what, until recently, would have been accepted as the norm. The following example highlights this point:

> A young obsessional man in his teens suffered from a fear of developing cancer and would assiduously avoid all activities that might expose him to carcinogens, including the sun, ambient air pollution, and avoiding the basement of the family house for fear of being exposed to gas, a rare cause of lung cancer. When family and friends suggested that his fears were extreme and unreasonable, he countered that *no* risk was worth taking and suggested that others might be well advised to adopt his position as well.

Rationalization is the primary cognitive strategy of obsessionals, and it is almost impossible to divest them of it. Rather than accept that their behaviors are irrationally fearful — which is the first and necessary step toward achieving a change — they will instead seek factual support for their behavior, as noted above with reference to the current pandemic. Complex rituals may develop to ward off potential danger magically. In this regard, although wearing a flimsy mask may help reduce exposure to aerosolized droplets in certain up close interactions with strangers, there is no data to suggest that it effectively protects one from viral spread. It is a talisman. Excessive fear limits experience, which is Shapiro's definition of neurosis.

Unfortunately, such levels of fearful concern are becoming increasingly commonplace. One sees them virtually everywhere as excessive anxiety around parenting, impolitic speech, and health. When such perfectionism becomes the norm, society may properly be termed neurotic.

Excessive existential insecurity is a source of shame. Shame is characterized by efforts at concealment, and this is how rationalization serves the obsessional, i.e., as a dimly conscious subterfuge meant to conceal his fear from others. Obsessionals that refuse to consider that their fears might be the cause of their rationalizations are judged as having "limited insight," which is a poor prognostic sign (*Diagnostic and Statistical Manual of Mental Disorders-V*, 2010). As personality styles are themselves addictive, genuine change is difficult to achieve (R. Kradin, 2008).

In some cases, when feelings of insecurity are highly defended against, it may be best not to disturb them in psychotherapy, as insight — if not carefully titrated — can result in the emergence of psychosis. The following is such an example:

A middle-aged obsessional man from a wealthy family was constantly engaged in lawsuits with his mother, brothers, and sister. These took up most of his mental energy and generally involved what for him were piddling sums of money. However, when it was suggested that this litigious behavior was, in fact, motivated by other factors and that he could afford to "lose the money" for the sake of familial harmony, he was incredulous that someone might even suggest the idea of losing even a small sum to a family member. He became deeply depressed, delusional, paranoid, and non-functional.

Some obsessionals are aware of their issues but use their intellect to distance themselves from their feelings. In psychotherapy, they may describe what is wrong with them with some accuracy, but with little feeling and, in the absence of being ill at ease, they have little motivation to change. They may openly admit their faults, but continue to harbor fantasies of perfection. To defend against exposure, they may prefer to offer up their "flaws" before they are discovered by the analyst. This constitutes a resistance to therapeutic progress and limits the efficacy of treatment:

> A 50-year-old man entered therapy with the goal of knowing more about himself. He insisted that he was not interested in exploring his past or any dystonic feelings that he might be experiencing despite having a host of problems in his life, including a host of compulsive activities. After several sessions, he announced that he had been giving matters a lot of thought on his own and now understood himself, so he would no longer require treatment.

The outcome of treatment came as little surprise as there was a strong resistance toward self-examination.

RESTRICTION OF AFFECT

Thought effectively limits the awareness and expression of affect. At a granular level, it is impossible to think and feel simultaneously. The non-neurotic mind fluidly alternates between thinking and feeling, whereas compulsive thinking reinforces the obsessional's restriction of affect. But it would be wrong to conclude that the obsessional is a "cold" character. In some contexts, he may display extraordinary sentimentality. One obsessional male patient routinely was moved to tears at parades and weddings. Others exhibit extraordinary sympathy toward those they perceive as disadvantaged. But, as will be discussed below, this is not empathy; rather it represents the projection of their own disavowed memories of rejection and abandonment.

The cool persona of the obsessional can often be traced to a childhood in which they were forced prematurely to assume an adult "parental" role. As such, obsessionals give the impression of being independent and competent which, in fact, they may be at the workplace or in managing the home. But they will complain of feeling overwhelmed and fear abandonment in close relationships. They can become resentful and spiteful when others do not attend to their needs.

A 54-year-old man was highly successful professionally. He came to analysis with marital difficulties, complaining that his wife was "cold" and unsupportive. Within the family, he often assumed the role of concerned caretaker for his young children and accused his wife of neglecting them. He was angry with his wife and resentful of feeling misunderstood and unrewarded by others, despite his success. He prided himself on being hyper-responsible but always felt on the verge of being overwhelmed and resented having to attend to the needs of others. He approached his divorce as another issue that needed to be managed but recognized that something was missing in his "heart."

ANGER

Freud recognized that the obsessional is angry with authority but takes great pains to conceal it, even from himself. In many cases, one encounters an early developmental situation in which anger directed at caretakers was rebuffed, or responded to, in turn, with anger, guilt-producing or shaming behaviors, or frank rejection. The parental home is often described as perfectionistic, tightly controlled, and a place where autonomy was discouraged. In other cases, it may have been sufficiently chaotic that all the child's energies needed to be directed at maintaining some degree of order. In such cases, the obsessional features tend to alternate with chaotic behaviors. Contradictory and confusing parental displays of enabling and abandoning behaviors are commonly reported.

> L. was raised by parents who both exhibited severe obsessional traits. Perfectionism was the mode in her rule-bound home and polite behavior without displays of anger were insisted upon. Whereas L. viewed her father as nurturing, analysis revealed that he was highly controlling and had persistently resisted L.'s efforts to act independently. Her mother was described as critical, distant, and prone to abandoning L. when she expressed any signs of anger.

This mode of parenting makes it extremely difficult for children to discern that they are being controlled or to develop genuine autonomy. As adults, they alternate between being overly reliant on authority or at odds with it.

Repressed anger at caregivers is carried into adult relationships, in which relationships to authority are conflicted. This manifests as sado-masochistic dynamics (Shapiro, 1981). Sado-masochistic attachments are often maintained until no further attachment benefit can be gleaned from them.

Anger, like other negative affects, is repressed and virtually impossible to access. To guise their feelings, some obsessionals develop an exceptionally gentle persona. But, when sufficiently challenged, they may erupt with displays of hostility. What is more commonly observed are unconsciously-driven *passive-aggressive* strategies aimed at frustrating and evoking anger in others. This is achieved by what Klein referred to as *projective identification* (Ogden, 2005). When this defense is successful, it manages to elicit expressions of anger in others, but one can often detect a faint sadistic smile on the face of the obsessional patient, who is gratified by seeing the object of the projective identification lose control while he maintains his own (Reich, 1962).

In public and in the face of authority, the obsessional is polite and even obsequious. But the attuned analyst can discern hints of anger in the form of sarcasm or facial expressions that reflect contempt (Reich, 1962). One obsessional patient would routinely crumple the check that he used for payment before handing it to me, as a manifestation of his otherwise well-hidden contempt.

The behavior of the obsessional in public can differ greatly from what is observed in private:

A husband in marital therapy noted that his wife was viewed as extraordinarily nice by the neighbors but prone to hysterical temper tantrums when behind closed doors. On one occasion, he related that the doorbell rang in the middle of a boisterous fight, and his wife transformed immediately back to the angelic persona that she reserved for strangers. After her brief encounter with the neighbor and as soon as the front door was closed, she immediately reverted to raging.

Jung frequently referred to the mild-mannered professor who was a raging tyrant at home.

The adult obsessional compulsively re-enacts the parental demand of behaving like a "nice" boy or girl. Indeed, this persists into adulthood and can become so overbearing as to eclipse all other concerns. One moody young man would smile when being photographed and then immediately revert to being unpleasant to his family. Around friends and strangers, he was consistently polite, gentle, and enthusiastic. At home, he was sullen, rude, and passive-aggressive. In public, the obsessional is careful to display inordinate sensitivity toward the feelings of others and may be widely viewed as "compassionate" or as a really "nice guy," both admirable qualities in theory.

Unfortunately, as Shapiro notes, these behaviors are, in fact, neurotic as they do not represent the genuine feelings of the obsessional:

> What makes the conscientiousness of the compulsive person special is different from the nature or the strength of his values, standards, or purposes.... When the compulsive person reminds himself that he should do something because it is the right thing, the nice thing, or the generous thing, he is prompted not by kindness, generosity, or concern for justice but by a sense of rules and duties to do something kind, generous, or nice (Shapiro, *Autonomy*, p. 80).

In private, the obsessional is more than willing to criticize others, especially those who do not share his values. He is also apt to adopt punitive measures toward others that cannot be traced directly to him. To maintain his "nice" ego-ideal, he must act covertly, protected from potential confrontations. This strategy contributes to the underlying psychology of "political correctness" and its appeal to obsessional society.

In institutional settings, committees are the preferred mechanism for obsessionals to express their hostility toward others without fear of retribution or having to be viewed publicly as "mean." As the obsessional personality fears losing control and becoming angry in public, direct confrontations with others are avoided. A highly obsessional young man was showered with faint praise by his peers as being the "least likely to confront someone." Attempts to avoid confrontation may involve deceitful behaviors. Many politicians at all levels of governance adopt this strategy, as they are practiced at deception in the service of avoiding confrontation and maintaining obsessional control.

In groups, obsessionals strive to create a "civil" environment of polite but shallow interactions. Kindness, a genuine virtue, is for the obsessional an imperative, as well as a meta-communication of personal vulnerability and hypersensitivity. When taken to the extreme, as it is today in classrooms and workplaces as "political correctness," it limits the ability to teach effectively. As Hillel, a Talmudic sage observed in the *Ethics of the Fathers*…the overly sensitive student cannot learn" (Lau, 2007).

Unfortunately, unpleasant situations at times must be addressed if they are to be remedied. In the 2016 presidential election, Progressive obsessionals chose to ignore the fact that there was overwhelming evidence to suggest that Hillary Clinton had a reputation of being dishonest and corrupt.[13] Had the Democratic establishment taken the opportunity to confront the truth about their chosen candidate, the outcome of the election may well have been different.

I learned as a young physician that addressing unpleasant situations was rarely the path chosen by administrators, who are accomplished at putting their "heads in the sand." Consider the following vignette:

A young physician was overwhelmed during a resuscitation effort of a severely ill patient in the emergency room. His medical decisions directly resulted in the patient's death. Out of control, he was uttering profanities during the ill-fated resuscitation effort. The next day he was summoned to the office of the hospital director where not a word concerning his medical mal-

13 It is not my goal here to discuss the various claims about political figures. However, for individuals such as the Clintons, who spent their lifetimes in politics to achieve personal wealth estimated in the tens of millions of dollars without participating in corruption should defy the common sense of anyone who has lived on this planet for any length of time. Requiring proof in the form of a "smoking gun" to reach this conclusion is why some lawyers/politicians engender so little respect from the decent common folk.

practice was mentioned; rather, he was severely dressed down for his use of profanity in front of the nursing staff.

I have witnessed numerous similar responses during my years in academic medicine. Ethics and concerns for patient welfare — as well as the ultimate welfare of trainees — are often of secondary concern compared to the avoidance of "unpleasantness." Ultimately, it is the illusion of being "nice" that drives obsessional decision making in the public arena.

The importance of repressed anger in what is transpiring today should be evident. The Progressive left views itself as virtuous, kind, and anti-violent except, of course, when its views are challenged. When they view it as safe to do so, which means when it concerns fighting Conservatives and the "Evil Orange Man," they act angrily, viciously, and without any evidence of compassion.

DOUBT

Neuroscientist Antonio Damasio suggests that the normal decision-making process requires knowing how one *feels* about the choice (Damasio, 2000). On a cautionary note, feelings are not the same as emotions; they are, instead, as Jung termed them, rational evaluations with respect to what is likely to be beneficial or not *vis a vis* the self. The capacity to make decisions is a *sine qua non* of genuine autonomy. But the obsessional is limited in this capacity by an inability to know how he feels. When one takes a detailed developmental history, one finds that decisions were often made for the obsessional and there was little opportunity for self-determination. Consequently, he may renege on his decisions, fearful of having made the wrong one, or look to others to make choices for him. The latter may be an older parental figure or a peer group. When no alternative is available, the obsessional will procrastinate.

The classical example of obsessional preoccupation in literature is Shakespeare's *Hamlet*, in which the protagonist struggles throughout the play trying to decide how and when to act to avenge his father's murder and the usurpation of what was rightfully his throne. Consider the following example from my psychoanalytical practice:

A 40-year-old obsessional woman needed to replace her old car that was in the shop for repairs more than out. For more than a year, she researched automobiles, looking for the "perfect choice." But each time she came close to deciding, she became paralyzed by doubt. After two years, she precipitously purchased a car that lacked most of the features she had been searching for.

This mode of manic decision making is also common for obsessionals. Eventually unable to tolerate the anxiety that accompanies being paralyzed by doubt, they make a sudden decision that does not serve them well, simply to get it out of the way. Freud recognized this failure to commit as a common feature of obsessionality.

PERFECTIONISM

The obsessional is by definition a perfectionist. But as "to err is human," obsessionals are prone to implosions of self-esteem when their flaws are exposed. To maintain the illusion of perfection, the obsessional must assiduously avoid criticism. This may include limiting their "interests" to the small numbers of activities they excel at while denigrating those that they do not. Exceptionally "thin-skinned," they see imperfections in others, but not in themselves. Alternatively, they may be excessively humble, quick to criticize themselves, and to ignore the faults of others. The latter strategy is invariably a ruse, meant to maintain their image of being "kind," although their own level of narcissistic absorption may not allow them even to register the faults of others. The ego defenses of obsessionals vary with their degree of psychological sophistication from crude denial to avoidance, repression, and projection. This obsessional proclivity is so ancient that it was exhibited in Genesis by Adam, who blamed Eve for his own moral failings, whereas Eve blamed the serpent.

Perfectionism is always a sign of psychological immaturity. The obsessional resembles Jean Piaget's description of the six-year-old child who still believes in perfectionism and the magical omnipotence of his thought (Piaget, 1960). Indeed, the analysis of the obsessional invariably uncovers puerile inclinations in many areas. For example, whereas they are often serious without much of a sense of humor, they may be amused by "bathroom humor" and by puns.[14]

A patient described his father as a severely obsessional personality. When the child was young, they would watch cartoons on television together. But, after the age of six or seven, the child grew tired of the silly images while his father continued to watch the cartoons by himself, chuckling all the while at what the boy had grown to view as inane.

Obsessional hypersensitivity to criticism leads to diminished risk taking and diminished creativity. Obsessionals' intense self-scrutiny and impossibly high standards result in a pervasive lack of joy, a state referred to as *anhedonia*, i.e., the inability to enjoy life.

---

14 The letters of Wolfgang Amadeus Mozart to his father Leopold and to his own wife include numerous allusions to bathroom activities and the extensive inclusion of puns.

CLEANLINESS

Most are acquainted with obsessionals who have a preoccupation with cleanliness. The classic example is the housewife who cleans compulsively, making certain that nothing "foreign" contaminates the purity of her domicile, or the patient with OCD who exhibits compulsive hand washing. For some obsessionals, the concern is with "dirt"; for others, it is exposure to germs. These two preoccupations often overlap. The underlying fear includes contamination, illness, and death.

If one considers the rigid barriers between unconscious process and consciousness, it is not surprising that obsessionals generate various boundaries to secure their well-being. One can imagine this unconscious strategy as a fractal that iterates itself repeatedly at different scales of experience.[15]

The obsessional tends to be uncomfortable with and, in severe cases, even repudiate, the body and the physical world. They are paradoxically at one level overly concerned with the material world; on the other, they reject it and tend to seek refuge in their own thoughts. Psychotherapists often must encourage the obsessional to "re-inhabit" his body.

The desire to purge the world of "dirt" extends to many levels of obsessional experience. Political correctness may be interpreted as an obsessional effort at purifying speech of "dirty" words and phrases that potentially stigmatize others. However, even Saul Alinsky, the political organizer and mentor of both Hillary Clinton and Barack Obama, bristled at the idea of expunging words with unpleasant connotations and rejected efforts at sterilizing speech. As he complains in *Radicals: A Primer for Realistic Radicals* (Alinsky, 1971):

---

15 A fractal is a self-reiterating function, much like a tree that continues to branch at both larger and smaller levels.

Let us look at the word *power*. *Power* meaning "ability, whether physical, mental, or moral, to act," has become an evil word, with overtones and undertones that suggest the sinister, the unhealthy, the Machiavellian. ...the word *power* is mentioned as though hell has been opened, exuding the stench of the devil's cesspool of corruption. It evokes images of cruelty, dishonesty, selfishness, arrogance, dictatorship, and abject suffering. The word *power* is associated with conflict; it is unacceptable in our present Madison Avenue deodorized hygiene, where conflict is blasphemous and the value is being liked and not offending others. *Power*, in our minds, has become almost synonymous with corruption and immorality (Alinsky, *Primer*, p. 51).

One could not ask for a better summary of the hypersensitive concerns of the obsessional Progressive. Power, contamination, politeness — Alinsky touches on all their major themes. Apparently, Alinsky's famous liberal mentees missed this point. Indeed, this radical's approach to language more closely approximates that of Donald Trump.

The desire to expunge the world of "dirt" may explain the environmental concerns of obsessional Progressives. Pollution due to carbon fuels is based less on well-established science than on the need to create "clean" energy. When coupled with a neurotic abhorrence of waste, one is left with absurd suggestions like the "Green New Deal," which would bankrupt America or any global economy for what can only be termed a fantasy. Indeed, the emphasis that obsessionals place on abstract modeling as opposed to real scientific data was recently evidenced by the predictions of how many would die in this country due to the coronavirus infection. The fact that the models grossly overestimated the death counts barely concerned Progressives. The absurd contradictions as to whether wearing masks is protective or not reflect the inconsistencies of obsessional so-called scientific experts.

IDÉE FIXEE (FIXED IDEAS)

The *idée fixee* was originally recognized as a feature of obsession-ality and is also seen in paranoid personalities. The afflicted person is unable to resist a train of thought. In neurosis, these compulsive thoughts are recognized as irrational, but in psychosis, they are accepted without dispute and the individual cannot be converted from his belief.

It is commonplace for Progressives to accuse Donald Trump of being a "racist." Despite virtually no credible evidence to support this claim, they refuse to be swayed by evidence to the contrary. To claim that half of the country is currently delusional may sound ludicrous, but the fact is that such fixed ideas suggest that there is a degree of psychotic ideation in America today that will not yield to reason.

An obsessional woman in her early 30s was the daughter of an Italian-American physician who died suddenly when she was in her 20s. She recalled many fond moments with her father but was disturbed by what she viewed as his "racism." She had a propensity to date African-American men, often far less intel-ligent and accomplished than herself. When I suggested that perhaps her choice of partners might be unconsciously driven by anger toward her father, she became irate and quit analysis, suggesting that she could not work with a "racist."

I have little doubt that this patient was correct in suggesting that her father likely held racial prejudices, as these were common and overt in his generation. But she admitted that he never acted in an overtly discriminatory way toward people of color. This distinction between thought and action is critical. In most societies, it is a fundamental tenet of the law that only actions are subject to punishment. But today's politically correct society is approaching George Orwell's *1984,* in which "thought crimes"[16] are subject to punitive action (Orwell, 1950). Whereas prejudicial speech *is* disturbing, in a liberal society in which the individual is granted the right of free speech, it should be permissible, and certainly one must retain the right to harbor private thoughts without recrimination. The fact is that we are all guilty of less than glowing opinions of some people or groups, but to hold individuals to impossible standards is symptomatic of neurotic perfectionism.[17] As political commentator David Horowitz suggests in *Progressive Racism*:

> To achieve the benevolent outcomes that progressives promise would require a government both omniscient and wise, a utopia that has never existed. Such a state would have to mandate comprehensive strategies of opportunity and wealth, and would conduct a relentless battle against human nature to overcome the resistance to its impositions by those unwilling to give up their liberty or the fruits of their labor.... The level playing field requires a totalitarian state to eliminate the disparities resulting from human nature and private circumstance (Horowitz, *Progressive*, p. 57).

Indeed, one of the most disturbing features of the current Progressive agenda is the collapse of thought, speech, and action into a singular

---

16 The basis of this may be traced to early Christianity. Many of the sayings attributed to Jesus in his sermon on the mount in Matthew and in the plain in Luke extend the transgression of the law from a mode of action to a mode of thought. The usual motif is that "you have been taught x, but I say y," with y being a more extreme element linked to thought preceding action. Sin becomes not merely a behavioral transgression, but a thought crime. A modern example is President Jimmy Carter's statement during an interview that he often "sinned in his heart."

17 In the opening discussion of the 18th CE text Tanya by the first *Rebbe* of Chabad chasidism, there is a lengthy discussion of what constitutes a pure *Tzaddik*, or righteous man, and a *beinoni*, that is, an in-between man. Both observe the Law perfectly and are indistinguishable to an observer. They differ in that the pure *Tzaddik* no longer has any inclination toward sin. It is noted that such people are extremely rare. To hold individuals to such an impossible standard leads to self-loathing and intolerance and one is chided not to think of oneself as a "bad person" lest one become depressed and unable to live a joyful life.

monolithic taboo on a wide variety of topics.

I genuinely doubt that this young woman was devoid of her own degree of prejudice, but unfortunately her hypersensitivity precluded the possibility of exploring that possibility, which she might have found enlightening. But her mindset has become the norm for obsessional Progressives, especially among "millennials,"[18] as a result of what has been systematic inculcation into Progressive ideology in schools, and peers on social media. Efforts to reserve one's individual rights and identity are routinely challenged in Progressive society:

> A young woman was approached by a black man for a date. For a variety of personal reasons, she refused. She was subsequently accused by the man and by her own friends of being a "racist" and pressured to go out on the date.

CONCRETE PERSPECTIVE AND LIMITED CREATIVITY

The perceptual field of obsessionals is narrow and, consequently, they tend to "miss the forest for the trees." They are well qualified to perform detailed tasks, and are often drawn to them. However, as their results must be "perfect," it can require lengthy periods of time for them to complete a task. A behavioral slowness permeates the obsessional's life, which may make him appear to be "stuck in the mud." One young obsessional man would take more than an hour to complete a simple meal, carefully cutting and slowly chewing his food.

Concrete thinking also characterizes obsessionals. They may have difficulty appreciating metaphors and symbolic thinking. They prefer questions with clear and preferably quantitative answers. They tend to eschew shades of grey and exhibit a limited ability to compromise on

---

18 Millennials are poorly defined as those who will become adults in the early 21ˢᵗ CE, including those born between the late 1980s and 2000.

matters when they think they are correct.

Creativity is arguably not the obsessional's forte. Rarely do they make paradigm-shifting discoveries. Instead, their ideas tend to rely on what is already well accepted, to which they may contribute small new elements. At times, they will unconsciously assume credit for the ideas of others, a phenomenon referred to as *cryptomnesia*, a form of unconscious plagiarism.

As a research fellow, I worked with a highly intelligent and obsessional mentor. During my research, I made a small but novel observation that I shared with him. He was immediately skeptical and showed little excitement about the discovery. Frustrated over time with his lack of enthusiasm, and recognizing the potential importance of the finding, I submitted the research for publication, having grown weary of waiting for his approval. The paper was rapidly accepted for publication in a quality scientific journal. Several months later, my mentor enthusiastically called me into his office to discuss a "new" finding that he had just read about. It was the very topic that I had discussed with him repeatedly but he apparently had no recollection of our discussions. When I inquired as to who had published it, he said that he would check the authorship and get back to me. He chose not to pursue the conversation when he realized that it had been published from his own laboratory.

Although perplexing and frustrating at the time, his behavior later became clarified when I saw reference to it some years later in a text on obsessionality. In it, psychoanalyst Leonard Salzman notes that obsessives tend not to believe new ideas unless they first read about them elsewhere. This reflects their over-reliance on authority (Salzman, 1977).

Due to their high intelligence, organizational, and political skills, obsessionals tend to rise to levels of leadership in organizations. Unfortunately, once there, they prefer to organize rather than to innovate. The result is too often an entrenched and inertial bureaucracy. With time, obsessional organizations tend to stagnate until new creative minds are brought in to "shake things up." People like Donald Trump, who are open to new approaches to solving problems, are anathema to obsessionals. In addition, for all the reasons noted above, Obsessionals are famously slow to act decisively. Envious of those who can, they tend to guise their envy with contempt.

An example of the conflict between personality types was publicly acted out between Trump and Dr. Anthony Fauci concerning how to approach the coronavirus pandemic. Fauci, a fixture in Progressive Washington, prides himself on being "scientific." But many of his suggested policies concerning the role of masks, lockdowns, and school closures have been based on virtually no scientific data. On the other hand, Trump, himself a confessed "germophobe," recognized the need to limit the spread of the virus while also maintaining public confidence, preserving a booming American economy, and rapidly developing an effective vaccine. Had Fauci been left to his obsessional druthers, a vaccine *might* have been developed sometime within the decade. But Trump succeeded in delivering *several* vaccines in less than a year, an unheard-of accomplishment and a credit to his common sense and insistence on cutting through the bureaucratic "red tape." Fauci's contempt for Trump's style has been evident in recent media interviews, as he unfortunately continues to "lead" the public health response to the pandemic from "behind."

ENVY AND SCHADENFREUDE

Perfection is not an achievement that the obsessional easily shares with others. Consequently, he is prone to be envious of anyone who achieves success. This is the psychological state the Germans referred to as *schadenfreude*. It is the inclination of the obsessional to demean anything good that might happen to others.

A highly intelligent and obsessional young man applied and was accepted to an Ivy League college. However, when he learned that his best friend had been accepted at the school of *his* choice, he was visibly upset and insisted that he could not have been accepted to an Ivy League university without the help of a financial "bribe" by his wealthy parents. He himself had been accepted as a "legacy" student.

This lack of generosity toward others is symptomatic of the pettiness of spirit of obsessionals. In today's climate, this is seen in the inability of Progressive politicians to credit Trump with any success and their continued blood lust for discrediting him, even after he has left office. His accomplishments with the economy and foreign affairs are either criticized or unacknowledged. Indeed, Progressives delighted in the unexpected decimation of the Trump economy by the coronavirus epidemic. They would rather see the country fail than admit that Trump has succeeded at any level — true schadenfreude. In this spirit of "kindness," they have insisted on impeaching Trump a second time *after* he has already left office.

AVERSION TO RISK AND CONFRONTATION

Rather than admit that others are less fearful, which would suggest imperfection, the obsessional is critical of risk takers, preferring to view them as "brash," or "cavalier." Should the risk taker succeed, he is *lucky*, as the obsessional rarely admits the talents of others. On the other hand, should the risk taker fail, the judgment that "he got his just desserts" is swift. Much of the aversion to Donald Trump expressed by obsessionals is attributable to his risk taking, which obsessionals view as dangerous, or as incompetent, despite the fact that he has repeatedly proven to be successful with his "risky" policies. When President Trump was first elected, obsessional elites predicted that the American economy would collapse. They were completely wrong. They said he would start a nuclear war. Wrong again. They have been wrong about virtually everything concerning Trump, but they will never admit it, as it only proves how incompetent they are.

HUMILITY

The obsessional is critical of himself and others. He may be self-deprecating and behave humbly, but this invariably is due to covert feelings of grandiosity. The latter may be the most difficult element to access in the treatment of the obsessional. Committed to being humble, the obsessional will adamantly deny his covert feelings of superiority to others. Indeed, the suggestion that the obsessional harbors substantial grandiosity will invariably evoke angry denials. The overt grandiosity of Donald Trump infuriates obsessionals who have spent their lives keeping their own narcissism under wraps.

POWER AND CONTROL

Power is a key issue for obsessionals. Social psychoanalyst Erich Fromm describes this in *Escape from Freedom*, in which he examines the *authoritarian personality,* which is essentially identical to the obsessional personality (Fromm, 1960). Fromm focuses primarily on the conflicts with respect to power and powerlessness that plague these individuals.

> Returning now to the discussion of the authoritarian character, the most important feature to be mentioned is its attitude toward power. For the authoritarian character there exists, so to speak, two sexes: the powerful ones and the powerless ones. His love, admiration, and readiness for submission are automatically aroused by power, whether of a person or an institution. Power fascinates him, not for any values for which a specific power may stand, but just because it is power. Just as his "love" is automatically aroused by power, so powerless people or institutions automatically arouse his contempt. The very sight of a powerless person makes him want to attack, dominate, humiliate him.

> There is one feature of the authoritarian personality which has misled many observers: a tendency to defy authority and to resent any kind of influence from above.... Sometimes the attitude toward authority is divided (Fromm, *Escape*, p. 167).

The developmental history of the obsessional often includes an authoritarian parent who made rigid demands of the child. Efforts at influencing the obsessional parent were unsuccessful, leaving the child frustrated and with a sense of powerlessness.

As an adult, the obsessional may be exquisitely attuned to power dynamics and compulsively seek to gain control over others so as not to relive childhood feelings of helplessness. If this cannot be achieved, passive/aggressive dynamics may emerge that covertly seek to frustrate the power of others. Due to unexpressed feelings of early frustration, they may show an underlying destructiveness unconsciously directed at the authoritarian parent. This can yield the impulse to destroy anything that reminds them of the authoritarian parental figure. Progressivism exhibits this underlying wish for destructiveness, but often offers no viable alternatives to replace it.

Perhaps no feature of obsessionals is more apparent to others than the need to control others. They insist on being in control in virtually all situations, and may become anxious and angry when the opportunity is denied them. As might be expected, obsessionals compulsively seek positions of leadership and political influence. Only when exerting power over others do they feel immune to being controlled. Control of others is Janus-faced; on one hand, it can lead to increased efficiency in carrying out an agenda, but when it stifles the autonomy of others, their willingness to cooperate is diminished and may evoke passive/aggressive strategies that serve to frustrate their uninvited power. The cry "to resist" the agenda of the Trump administration is such an example, although the perception of the overbearing power exerted by the president was grossly exaggerated.

The analysis of the obsessional reveals repeated childhood impingements on autonomy. There is an optimal degree of personal space that individuals require for normal development that varies between individuals. It may account for the misattuned interactions of some mothers and infants. Impingements develop through intrusions into both the psychological and physical domains of the child, and they are generally initiated by an anxious, controlling mother. As psychoanalyst Donald Winnicott suggests:

Maternal failures produce phases of reaction to impingement and these reactions interrupt the "going on being" of the infant. An excess of this reacting produces not frustration but a threat of annihilation. This, in my view, is a very real primitive anxiety, long antedating any anxiety that includes the word death in its description (D. Winnicott, 1966)

Repeated impingements are experienced as traumatic and, when perceived as re-experienced by adults, can trigger anxiety, anger, and despair.

The experience of the impinged-upon child alternates between feeling overly scrutinized and ignored. The result is a profound sense of insecurity, a compulsive need to control one's self and others, and a deeply embedded conviction that others can neither be trusted nor of help. These adults may compulsively seek caretaking behaviors but ultimately reject them with a pseudo-independent aloofness. They represent "help-rejecting complainers" who will invariably refuse to accept help when offered (R. Kradin, 2008; "Psychological Healing: A Historical and Clinical Study." Vol. I. London: George Allen and Unwin, 1925).

Obsessional parenting styles have become commonplace, especially among educated individuals in America. Steeped in the "culture of the therapeutic" and influenced by maternal styles fostered by feminism, young children are being raised by "helicopter" parents who insist on providing the "perfect" environment for their young children. The result has been a disastrous increase in narcissistically disturbed and obsessional young adults who are ill prepared for dealing with the unavoidable traumas and disappointments of adult life. Help-seeking behaviors have become a well-recognized phenomenon on university campuses. Young students, insecure and narcissistically fragile, insist on being provided with an environment that will ensure their safety from perceived dangers. But their perception of adversity is negative in the extreme. Their behavior is immature and entitled and, whereas their concerns should be empathically addressed, they should not be indulged.

Unfortunately, this is not the reigning opinion of Progressive educators who yield to, and even encourage their demands. But if the actual source of their anxieties is not identified and appropriately confronted — which is the accepted treatment for anxiety-driven phobias — these young people will never be able to manage real-world challenges on their own. Teachers and university administrators who enable these behaviors will bear responsibility for having created a lost generation and for undermining America's future.

FAIR AND BALANCED

The obsessional mind is preoccupied with fairness. This may manifest as a concern for not exhibiting preferences. When it comes to money, the obsessional may go to extremes to appear fair. This often takes the form of exactly dividing a check when dining out, or making certain that everyone shares equally in the tipping. They are unlikely to be sufficiently generous to offer to pick up a check.

Even minimal disorder can be disturbing for the obsessional. This may be directed at the careful arrangement of furniture — often sparse — or the orderly arrangement of money in a billfold, or the avoidance of any situation that might potentially get out of control.

In their interactions with others, obsessionals adopt a "tit for tat" reaction to perceived slights. They have a long memory for having been insulted and will seek opportunities for reprisals. Cooperation between obsessionals is difficult as they are prone to power struggles. But what is most crucial for the obsessional is achieving a "perfect" moral stance.

CHAPTER 3: MORALITY AND THE OBSESSIONAL

I know not whether Laws be right or whether Laws be wrong...

— Oscar Wilde, *Ballad of Reading Gaol*

The political conflict in America today is in large measure a culture war. As will be argued here, the culture wars are, in turn, reflections of differences in the interpretation of the Judeo-Christian ethic. Traditionally, American morality has been rooted in the Judeo-Christian ethic for religionists and secular Americans alike. As philosopher Jurgen Habermas emphasizes (Habermas, 1981; Habermas & Ratzinger, 2006):

> For the normative self-understanding of modernity, Christianity has functioned as more than just a precursor or catalyst. Universalistic egalitarianism, from which spring the ideals of freedom and a collective life in solidarity, the autonomous conduct of life and emancipation, the individual morality of conscience, human rights, and democracy is the direct legacy of the Judaic ethic of justice and the Christian ethic of love (Habermas, *Dialects*, p. 11).

As polymath Yale scholar David Gelernter argues, the Puritan founders of this country were steeped in both the New Testament and the Hebrew Bible (Gelernter, 2007). They derived meaning from the comparison of their entry into the New World and the ancient Israelites entering the Promised Land. In addition to their Christian belief in love of their fellowman, they revered Judaism's ethic of social justice. Judaism deems obedience to the law as a discipline, and as the path to diminished narcissistic preoccupation. It also values a tradition based on kinship and particularism. It is the template for Sowell's constrained vision.

Christianity is a syncretistic melding of Judaism and Hellenistic[19] philosophy. As sociologist Robert Nisbet states, "The Greeks, above any people known to us in antiquity, were fascinated by change, its sources, properties, directions, and its relation to the principles of organic growth" (Nisbet, 1969). Progress and rationality were the aims of Hellenistic philosophy. Unlike Judaism, Hellenism fostered a universalist ethic that argued against the accepted distinctions between men in the ancient world. This attitude was adopted by Christianity. As Paul argues in Galatians 3:28, "There is neither Jew nor Gentile, neither slave nor free, nor is there male and female, for you are all one in Christ Jesus." Nevertheless, Christianity held out little hope for salvation for those who did not share its vision; its universal vision went only so far.

As a reform movement in 1st CE Judaism, early Christianity aspired to break with Judaic Law. This tendency toward anomia in the early Church is evidenced by Paul's argument in Romans 7:

It was the Law that showed me my sin. I would never have known that coveting is wrong if the Law had not said, "You

---

19 Hellenism refers to the philosophy spread throughout much of the known world beginning in the 4th BCE in the wake of Alexander the Great's conquests. Alexander, having been mentored by Aristotle, envisioned a world universally immersed in Greek language and philosophy.

must not covet." But sin used this command to arouse all kinds of covetous desires within me! If there were no law, sin would not have that power. At one time, I lived without understanding the Law. But when I learned the command not to covet, for instance, the power of sin came to life, and I died. So, I discovered that the Law's commands, which were supposed to bring life, brought spiritual death instead.

But the Law was not simply an aspect of Judaism. It was the basis for what theologian J.D.G. Dunn has described as *covenantal nomism*. The Law was critical for how Jews were expected to live a moral life. As Dunn notes: "When it comes to differentiation within Judaism, the boundary markers were bound to be precisely those points of disagreement over *halakah* (laws), over covenantal nomism: how to live as a devout and faithful Jew. Hence the exaggerated emphasis on calendar, legitimate priesthood, and on ritual purity..." (Dunn, 1991). Thus, changes in Law would be expected to serve as the boundaries between the Pharisaic Judaism that Paul rejected and the new Christian sect.

It is not far-fetched to suggest that America was also founded on the premise of covenantal nomism. Indeed, the Mayflower Compact of the Pilgrims was such a document, and the Declaration of Independence and subsequent U.S. Constitution defined America as a secular expression of covenantal nomism, which established American identity. Progressives argue that the failure to represent women, blacks, and other aggrieved minorities void the validity of the covenant. But these issues have been addressed due to the ability of the law to adjust to the times. As Dunn notes, *covenantal nomism* of Judaism was not fixed; it included recognition that the Law "derived from and referred primarily to a different age and to different situations...there was a need to expound and elaborate the simpler rules and principles to take account of the complexities of daily life" (p. 130). The U.S. Constitution also provides this flexibility and has adapted to change. But this is not sufficient for left-wing Progressives, who seek to "transform America." If their aggressive efforts to undermine America by attacking the covenantal basis of the nation are not stopped peacefully, it will eventually lead either to a hot war for America's future identity, or a final "Parting of the Ways," with the rending of America into factions.

MESSIANISM

As historian of religion Gershom Scholem suggests, eschatological messianism is generally accompanied by anomic impulses, which must be reinterpreted when the expected end times do not materialize (Scholem, 1995). Paul, who unquestionably believed that he was living at the end of times, found it necessary to modify his message to the Corinthians when he learned they were ignoring the organizing rules of society. In brief, early Christianity preached the primacy of the spirit and viewed the Law as an unwelcome constraint. Christianity is the essential template for Sowell's unconstrained vision.

However, as Christianity became increasingly institutionalized, its initial anomic impulses were replaced by a new set of legalisms. By the 16th CE, Martin Luther, a young German Augustinian monk, found himself plagued with guilt and concerns for his own salvation, due to concerns with meeting the expectations of Christian law. In the psychobiography *Young Man Luther*, psychoanalyst Erik Erikson describes Luther as a classical obsessional neurotic (Erikson, 1995). Like Paul centuries before, Luther alleviated his guilt by restoring the idea of faith as the source of salvation and eliminating the need for the prescribed "works" of Roman Catholicism.

As Protestantism evolved, interest in the "Old Testament" was rekindled. The mythic characters of Abraham, Isaac, Jacob, Moses, and David became role models for faithful Protestants, and societal order became an increasing part of the Protestant vision. There was the emergence of a strong belief in predestination in Calvinism that fostered an intense work ethic which, as philosopher Max Weber suggested, laid the foundations for capitalism, the nation state, scientific exploration, and ultimately secularism (Weber, 2002).

Until recently, obsessional guilt was attributable to perceived transgressions of the Judeo-Christian ethic. But, since the 1960s, liberal Progressivism in America has undergone a transformation, one increasingly antagonistic to the rule of law and, like early Christianity, focused primarily on issues of social justice, most notably perceptions of racism, misogyny, and the mistreatment of illegal aliens. Modern Progressives view themselves as compassionate defenders of the disenfranchised. In this regard, they are currently supported by Pope Francis, who has broken with Catholic tradition by actively encouraging Progressive views on subjects ranging from homosexuality to global warming (Neumayr, 2017).

However, Progressive perceptions of who is disenfranchised are not necessarily supported by factual evidence. For example, in America there are increasing numbers of educated middle class and well-to-do blacks, as well as people of color serving at the heights of American government. Since the 1960s, white America has opened its doors to people of color. There is less overt prejudice than ever before, and less than virtually anywhere else in the world, including Africa. But these facts are consistently ignored by Progressives as inconvenient to their ideology, and they continue to assert that America is a racist nation (Horowitz, 2016).

The obsessional experiences guilt for what he perceives as his own moral imperfection. But what obsessional Progressives fail to perceive is that it is their *own* neurotic "victimhood" that they project onto those whom they view as vulnerable:

> A 48-year-old obsessional woman was the mother of a young boy with a modest but non-debilitating physical disability. She would present dreams where both she and a child were under attack from evil apocalyptic forces. In these dreams, it was her role to protect the child. Her own childhood had been harsh and she was both mentally and physically neglected.

This dream includes an archetypal image of a mother protecting her child. A comparable image is seen in the New Testament *Book of Revelation*. Certainly, the desire of a mother to protect her child is natural. But the parenting of today's Progressives exhibits pervasive obsessional concerns.

Obsessionals want to be cared for like the children they were never allowed to be. Often hard-working and responsible since childhood, they yearn to be unburdened of responsibility. But, unable to depend on others, they are instead neurotically compelled to protect those around them. This accounts for the coddling of their own children and their inordinate concern for those groups they see as disadvantaged. Enveloped in a web of illusions, they are unable to recognize and withdraw their projections. The obsessional is sincere but dishonest.

Concerns for the vulnerable and disenfranchised in society are not new. One of the great ethical advances of Judaism was a code of laws that made provisions for widows, orphans, the poor, and aliens. The ancient Israelites were repeatedly cautioned by the Law to recall that they were once "strangers in a strange land" and slaves in Egypt.[20] Ancient biblical Law also calls for measured and humane modes of punishment for legal infractions, as compared to the literal "eye for an eye" of the older codes of the Levant.[21]

Calls for social justice reached their zenith in the writings of rebuke of the ancient Israelite prophets. The prophetic tradition of social justice, especially the books of Isaiah, in turn, formed the basis for Jesus's teachings and those of the early Church.[22] But the teachings of Jesus were ideologically extreme with respect to most other sects of Second Temple Judaism. In his Sermon on the Mount — or on the Plain, depending on whether one refers to Matthew or Luke — Jesus suggests that one is as culpable for sinful thoughts as for sinful acts, thus holding man to a perfectionist morality that had never been practiced in Judaism. But it is important to recognize that Jesus believed that the *Kingdom of God* was nigh, which would profoundly transform man and other aspects of nature. To prepare for this, a higher level of moral perfectionism was required.

As Nietzsche noted, Christianity extols a perfectionistic moral standard that can undermine the success of society when adopted as the expected norm (Nietsche, 2017). Genuine morality is dependent on a profound degree of self-honesty and prone to distortion by self-deception. As Nietzsche suggested in a pre-psychoanalytical world:

---

20 The Law as used here and referred to in the New Testament is the Hebrew *Torah*, which is derived from a Hebrew root *hrh* that means instruction. The *Torah* includes the five books of Moses. The entire Jewish Law, which may not have been practiced in the 1st CE, includes the Oral Law and 613 Commandments, 365 proscriptions and 248 positive commandments. Since many pertained to the Temple cult, the current number is far smaller, although they are all considered topics for study in Rabbinic Judaism.

21 Despite biblical phrases that call for punishments that include an "eye for an eye, a tooth for a tooth," etc., the law has been consistently interpreted since antiquity as requiring monetary payments rather than physical body parts in civil cases. The driving idea is that the punishment should fit the crime and not be barbaric and extreme.

22 There are multiple references in the Gospels to the Hebrew prophets and in particular to the Book of Isaiah.

In helpful and benevolent people one nearly always finds a clumsy cunning that first rearranges the person who is to be helped so that, for example, he 'deserves' their help, needs their help and will prove to be deeply grateful, dependent, subservient for all their help. With fantasies such as these they control the needy like a piece of property.... (Nietzsche, *On Genealogy*, p. 194).

This aptly describes the mindset of today's Progressives and supports their Conservative detractors who argue that Progressivism fosters dependency and undermines human potential.

An example of such a laudable yet impractical standard of imposed utopian psychology, when applied in a hostile world, occurred on the Indian subcontinent under the rule of *Ashoka*, the king of the Indian Maurya Dynasty in the 3rd BCE. This Vedic warlord underwent a personal transformation due to feelings of guilt for the bloodshed in his military campaigns. He adopted the peaceful and compassionate tenets of Buddhism for himself and his kingdom.[23] Various extant stone stele monuments were erected by Ashoka. They promote peaceful co-existence and the abhorrence of anger and violence. But, following his death, Ashoka's kingdom reverted to its original warlike ways to protect itself from the persistent hostilities of its non-Buddhist neighbors.

English writer H.G. Wells noted in his *Outline of History*: "Amidst the tens of thousands of names of monarchs that crowd the columns of history, their majesties and graciousnesses, and serenities and royal highnesses and the like, the name of Ashoka shines, and shines, almost alone, a star" (Wells, 2004). But Wells was clear that unilateral placidity in a hostile world is also fraught with danger.

---

23 Those who study comparative religion, including Joseph Campbell, have envisioned Buddhism as an effort to escape from the present world, and therefore not a pragmatic theosophy to apply to pragmatic daily life. In Buddhism, a professional group of monastics practice meditative Buddhism, whereas the rest of the community gains merit by supporting them.

In his *Time Machine*, he imagined a future when humanity would be divided into two groups: the *Eloi* who, while highly morally evolved, were incapable of protecting themselves from the *Morlocks*, a primitive hostile group that preyed upon the undefended *Eloi* at will. This is the risk the West assumes in adopting pacifist ideas in a dangerous world, failing to recognize this is masochistic and potentially self-defeating. As Freud noted in *Mourning and Melancholia*, the obsessional is prone to masochistic behaviors (S. Freud, 1959).

What in fact protects individuals and nations, as America's Founding Fathers recognized, is not the questionably well-intentioned charity or compassion of others, but the rule of law and the ability to defend against those who want to do harm. Charity and compassion are too often idiosyncratically tainted by misguided intentions to be a guiding principle for government. After all, how is one reliably to discern what is genuine compassion from unconscious neuroticism?

The Hebrew Bible insists that one must not mistreat the disadvantaged, but it sets out specific rules as to how this should be done. It does not suggest that the disadvantaged should be judged by a different set of standards than the rest of society. As it says in Leviticus 11:27, "You shall do no unrighteousness in judgement; you shall not respect the honor of the poor, nor honor the person of the mighty; but in righteousness you shall judge your neighbor." It does not advocate that one element of society place itself at a disadvantage for another to achieve social or economic equity or to assuage ill-conceived feelings of guilt. But this differs from the precepts of early Christianity and even from the positions espoused by the current Pope.

THE GOLDEN RULE

The standard of the Judeo-Christian ethic is often distilled to the "Golden Rule." Judaism phrases the Golden Rule differently than Jesus does in the Gospels. The Judaic form of the Rule is apodictic, i.e., "Do *not* do unto others what you do *not* want done to yourself," as opposed to the Christian dictum, "Do unto others what you want done to yourself." The former phrasing emphasizes protecting the individual rather than imposing self-determined ideas of what is "good" for another. Too many have suffered and died from well-intentioned Christian love, and many are still suffering today from the "compassion" of Progressivism, as will be discussed.

The Golden Rule has been critically examined by scholars. According to philosopher Marcus Singer in the *Golden Rule* (Neusner & Chilton, 2009), "The nearly universal acceptance of the golden rule and its promulgation by persons of considerable intelligence, though otherwise of divergent outlooks, would...seem to provide some evidence for the claim that it is a universal ethical truth" (Neusner, *Golden*, p. 2). But ethicist Bernard Gert in the same text avers:

> ...The Golden Rule is not really a very good rule of conduct....
> If followed literally, and how else are we to understand it, it requires all normal policemen not to arrest criminals, and all normal judges not to sentence them.... The Golden Rule also requires, and students might like this, that teachers not give flunking grades to students even if they deserve it (Neusner, *Golden,* p. 3).

Indeed, there are many Americans who would agree with Gert's concerns about the Golden Rule.

There are areas in America today where laws purposefully go unenforced and judges are reticent to impose "harsh" sentences on guilty criminals. In many institutions of higher learning, as I noted in my introduction, students, not teachers, have the final say with respect to curriculum and grades. Or, as Gert suggests, grades have been done away with altogether, so as not to offend those who do not do well, either for lack of applying themselves or genuinely diminished intellectual capacity.

Sigmund Freud expressed little enthusiasm for the Golden Rule, which he examined in *Civilization and its Discontents* (S. Freud, 1930). He viewed it as psychologically unrealistic because it requires the repression of the instinctive basis of love. It devalues love by failing to discriminate between those one feels genuine affection for and those one does not. He saw it as unjust because the character of most men is innately flawed, selfish, and hostile, so that it puts one at a disadvantage with respect to those not inclined to reciprocate. Whereas Jesus argues in Matthew 5:38 that one should "Turn the other cheek" to the hostility of others, Freud strongly disagrees. According to Freud:

> Civilization pays no attention to all this; it merely admonishes us that the harder it is to obey the precept, the more meritorious it is to do so. But anyone who follows such a precept in present-day civilization only puts himself at a disadvantage vis-à-vis the person who disregards it (Freud, *Civilization*, p. 143).

Freud viewed the Christian version of the Golden Rule as "other worldly." As he wrote:

> "At this point, the ethics based on religion introduces its promises of a better afterlife. But so long as virtue is not rewarded here on earth, ethics will, I fancy, preach in vain." (Neusner & Chilton, 2009).

Although Freud was an atheist, he was also a self-confessed ethnic Jew and, as I have argued elsewhere, much of his thought can be traced to tenets of Rabbinic Judaism (R. Kradin, 2016). As Phillip Rieff argues in *Freud: The Mind of the Moralist*, Freud expected that psychoanalysis would eventually replace religion as the basis of morality (Rieff, 1979). However, what he failed to perceive, or alternatively refused to admit, was that psychoanalysis was ultimately rooted in the morality of Judaism, and specifically in its notions of negation, which deny gratification of egotistical desires. Individual responsibility was the key to Freud's mature psychology, much as it is in Judaism.

Contrast Freud's pessimistic "realism" with the ideas of German 18th CE Christian philosopher Immanuel Kant (Kant, 1780). Kant conceived of a moral *categorical imperative* based on pure reason and devoid of feelings — a typical obsessional approach — in which man is compelled to adopt the highest moral stance regardless of reciprocity or the lack of desire of others to be treated as such. For Kant, abstract morality was the highest virtue, and all men were required to behave rationally and honestly despite the effect that it might have on others, even if it proved deleterious. Kant's idealistic perspective is at odds with Freud's pragmatism, and their underlying religious differences may account for this.

But, as Rieff notes in *Triumph of the Therapeutic*, the tenets of responsible morality are being replaced in America by the therapeutic mindset of Progressivism, in which immoral action is considered the result of psychopathology that requires therapy rather than punishment (Rieff, 1966). According to Rieff, it is somehow assumed in Progressive society that disadvantaged individuals have suffered some mode of developmental abuse or are the victims of racism and bigotry. Violent criminals, they argue, are the victims either of harsh upbringings, economic deprivation, or both. Virtually any physical or mental imperfection is termed a disability. Individuals are asked to bear no responsibility for their condition. Yet many who have grown up under difficult circumstances, even those who are seriously physically impaired, have become productive members of society.

The truth is that the "poor" are a heterogeneous group that includes those who are disabled, mentally lacking in the skills required to perform productive work, who prefer to make little effort in life and be supported by others, and those who make every effort to better their situation. Yet, for elite Progressives who know nothing about this firsthand, distinctions hardly matter; instead, all are considered equally disadvantaged and viewed as in need of government assistance.

Steven Sondheim's lyrics in the tune "Officer Krupke" in the 1957 American urban adaptation of Shakespeare's Romeo and Juliet, *West Side Story*, captures the opposing perspectives of Conservatives and Progressives on culpability. In the song's lyrics, a juvenile delinquent is shuffled back and forth between the police, magistrates, psychiatrists, and social workers without any clarity as to who has the authority to rule on his fate. In Progressive America, negation has been all but abrogated and replaced by enablement and gratification in an ill-conceived effort at preserving self-esteem rather than recognizing that genuine responsibility, which includes experiencing honest regret, guilt, shame, culpability, punishment, and atonement, is the only moral stance that can ultimately preserve and improve the fabric of society.

GOOD AND EVIL

Traditional Judaism and some Protestant sects comfortably embrace the ethical importance of law. They adopt "Old Testament" values that include both love and fear (awe) of God as the ultimate source of morality. The 16th CE Kabbalistic concept of the Godhead, and its subsequent Hasidic adaptation as a precursor of modern psychology, emphasizes the requirement for both "love" *(chesed)* and "limitation" *(gevurah)*. Whereas evil is said to derive from excessive limitation, unbounded love is frowned on. The co-expression of both "good" and "evil" within the Godhead are, in fact, essential requirements of genuine monotheism. As Isaiah 45:7 states, "I am the Lord, I create good *and* evil." The alternative to this stance leads to a radical duality that ascribes all "Good" to God as in the Augustinian theological position of God as *summum bonum* and all "Evil" as its Satanic counterpart. Such radical duality was part of apocalyptic sects in the times of the Second Temple, including the Jewish Qumran sect (Dead Sea sect) and early Jewish Christianity.

Like an apocalyptic sect, the obsessional psyche is structured as a radical duality. Good and bad are experienced in black-and-white terms, with little room for grey. This allows obsessionals to believe that they are the guardians of what is "good" while repressing "evil" and projecting it onto others. This is a dangerous psychology, as it fosters violent reactions toward those holding opposing views. A genuine "religious war" is transpiring in America between those who hold opposing visions of what is "good." Although both sides are secular, they are being driven by different sectarian accents of the Judeo-Christian ethic, each holding its position with ardent conviction.

As Dunn argues:

The significance of all this becomes clearer thanks to the insights of sociology and social anthropology — particularly with regard to the role of conflict in group self-definition. In order to form and maintain their identity, groups have to differentiate themselves from other groups. The closer other groups are to them and the more alike to them, the more important to define the boundary between them. Where the groups are close or very similar, the conflict is likely to be more intense: it is the brother who threatens identity most (the well-known phenomenon of sibling rivalry); it is the party most like your own which threatens…. (Dunn, p. 139).

Freud termed this phenomenon the "narcissism of minor differences." The truth is that, as unlike each other as American Progressives and Conservatives may be, they share far more in common with each other than with those living in China, Venezuela, or Norway.

A secular society, motivated by unconstrained "love" and concerns for the disenfranchised, and willing to forego the rule of law, errs by "throwing out the baby with the bath water," and sets the stage for the potential unraveling of society. In Freudian psychoanalysis, and for those who have studied infant development, it is evident that boundaries and limit setting are required for normal development. The failure to restrict gratification of the child does not lead, as some have erroneously concluded, to adults with improved self-esteem; rather, it is a recipe for narcissistic entitlement and for a precarious sense of self-worth. Discipline is required to achieve a mature sense of self and an internalized moral compass. Whereas "Love," as Paul suggests in 1 Corinthians 13:13, may be the highest ethical aspiration, it is potentially problematic unless one can distinguish true love from artefact, and few are in a position to do that accurately.

The Rabbinic sages were primarily concerned with a system of priestly purity laws that pertained only to Jews, but they did not ignore the moral obligations of the non-Jewish world. The so-called seven *Noachide Laws* were judged to be the minimal requirements to establish a stable society. The first tenet of the Noachide rules calls on non-Jews to create a system of courts to legislate and enforce laws. Disrespect for ruling government was seen as fundamentally immoral. Chapter 3:2 of the Talmudic tractate, *Ethics of the Fathers*, states: "Pray for the integrity of the government; for were it not for the fear of its authority, a man would swallow his neighbor alive"(Lau, 2007). Despite Roman antipathy toward the Jews at the time, the Rabbinic sages realized that laws were essential for preserving a healthy society.

But, in America today, there is an emerging and disturbing perspective on the part of some Progressives that the rule of law is optional when it conflicts with what they view as ethical "progress." But secular humanism offers no form of morality that is not ultimately rooted in the Judeo-Christian ethic (Habermas & Ratzinger, 2006). The only question is whether one adopts a pragmatic, religious-based morality that includes elements of responsibility or a utopian, compassionate morality that has never succeeded in this world. If there is doubt concerning this fact, one need only examine the abundant statistics that show what has happened to poverty and crime in the inner cities, the deterioration of performance on educational testing, and the lack of civility on university campuses since the 1960s, when the liberal Progressive agenda was widely adopted (C. Murray, 1984).

Habermas has suggested that the basis of a moral society is interactive dialog (Habermas & Ratzinger, 2006). But post-modernist ideas of morality prove that it is relative and without an innate compass. In theory, one is entitled to invent one's own moral standards, and no one has a legitimate right to question them. But this is an untenable operative definition of morality because it precludes the possibilities of meaningful dialogue and societal cohesion. Ultimately, it is solipsism, which is the opposite of morality. Calls to defund the police in Progressive cities suggests how divorced they have become from reality.

CHAPTER 4: LAW AND RELIGION IN AMERICA

All human things are subject to decay and, when fate summons, monarchs must obey.

— John Dryden, *Mac Flecknoe*

The Founding Fathers were aware that times change and that human laws are not immutable. To address this, they instated procedures for how the Constitution could be changed in the future, while safeguarding the intent of the original document. The Founders' approach resembles that of Rabbinic Judaism, which argues in favor of building a "fence around the Law" to preserve its sanctity (Lau, 2007).

If a consensus exists that the Constitution requires change, the Founders instituted a process for how this was to be achieved via legislation and the electorate. Judges were specifically excluded from the process, as their proper role is to interpret law, not to create it. Whereas some Progressive legal scholars argue that all interpretation is an act of "creation," the discriminating judge must discern the difference impartially. In this regard, the Hebrew Bible cautions judges not to stray in their objectivity when judging the rich and the poor. As Leviticus 24:22 states: "You are to have the same Law for the foreigner and the native-born. I am the LORD your God." The Law should apply equally without exception.

Nor is it the Constitutional role of the Executive branch of government to create laws by fiat. Rather, it is charged with the enforcement of laws already in place and with the protection of America's citizens. Executive orders may become *de facto* law but they are to have no permanent standing and may be undone by another Executive fiat or a court challenge.

Until recently, there has been an American truism that those who flouted the law would be subject to prosecution and punishment. In a country of law, "illegality" cannot be reconciled with what is "legal"; that is a *non sequitur*. The inability of Progressives to accept that aliens who arrive here illegally should be subject to deportation reveals the confusion of obsessional ideologues. Despite their black-and-white thinking, they paradoxically make room for what is "legal" and "illegal" to exist side by side without apparent incongruity. Most political Conservatives label this hypocrisy, but this assumes a level of awareness that may not be operative. Obsessional defenses tend to rigidly compartmentalize ideas and feelings that are irreconcilable. They ignore inconsistencies in their ideas if they conflict with their moral ideology. When confronted with the irrationality of their positions, they will deny them, change the subject, or denigrate those who question them. This serves to passive aggressively frustrate rational opponents and puts an abrupt end to dialogue.

For some Progressives, lying is also justified in the service of imagined moral superiority. When confronted with a clear transgression of Canon law, Pope Francis responded, "Who am I to judge?" This may sound Christ-like but it also makes a shambles of Church law. Pope Francis, who has avowed socialist leanings, promotes open borders, the rights of homosexuals, and an end to global warming. He is a darling of the Progressive left (Neumayr, 2017).

OBSESSIONALITY AND RELIGION

America is a large country with diverse values. A 2016 Gallup poll indicates that most Americans identify with a religious denomination (Poll, 2016). Indeed, some have suggested that religious affiliation is on the increase. However, only a minority of Americans actively practice their religion. In addition, polls suggest that 78% of Americans judge the level of morality in the country as poor and actively in decline, a huge statement about today's society. There can be little doubt that the decline in religious belief is a factor in the perceived moral decline, a topic elucidated in dialogue between the philosopher Habermas and the theologian Joseph Ratzinger (Pope Benedict XVI) (Habermas & Ratzinger, 2006).

Freud noted a substantial similarity between the thoughts and rituals of obsessionals and practicing religionists (S. Freud, 1907).

It is easy to see where the resemblances lie between neurotic ceremonials and the sacred acts of religious ritual: in the qualms of conscience brought on by their neglect, in their complete isolation from all other actions (shown in the prohibition against interruption), and in the conscientiousness with which they are carried out in every detail. But the differences are equally obvious, and a few of them are so glaring that they make the comparison a sacrilege: the greater individual variability of [neurotic] ceremonial actions in contrast to the stereotyped character of rituals (prayer, turning to the East, etc.), their private nature as opposed to the public and communal character of religious observances; above all, however, the fact that, while the minutiae of religious ceremonial are full of significance and have a symbolic meaning, those of neurotics seem foolish and senseless. In this respect an obsessional neurosis presents a travesty, half comic and half tragic, of a private religion. But it is pre-cisely this sharpest difference between neurotic and religious ceremonial which disappears when, with the help of the psy-cho-analytic technique of investigation, one penetrates to the true meaning of obsessive actions (Freud, *Obsessive Actions and Religious Practice*, p.119).

Indeed, prior to the emergence of psychology as an area of secular scholarship, obsessionality was primarily seen in the form of religious scrupulosity. The behaviors of many religious personalities, e.g., Martin Luther, would today undoubtedly be considered obsessional neurosis by secular psychologists (Erikson, 1995). However, to conclude that scrupulous religious individuals are neurotic is simplistic, as William James noted in his magisterial *Varieties of Religious Experience* (James, 2019). Only when behaviors are rooted in self-deception can they be judged neurotic. A deeply religious individual is acting out of profound belief, whereas the neurotic obsessional simply *acts*.

Teasing out neurosis from sincere religious beliefs is challenging but possible. Psychoanalyst Donald Winnicott once told a group of monastics who consulted him concerning the mental health of a mem-ber of their religious order that, if they felt "bored" in his presence, he was likely neurotic or worse. Mentally ill neurotics rarely act spontane-ously and consequently are experienced by others as tedious (Morris, 2016).

MORALITY

In *A Natural History of Morality*, Michael Tomasello suggests that morality emerged from a mammalian drive for interdependence (Tomasello, 2016). He notes:

The first (level of cooperation) is simply the cooperative pro-clivities of great apes in general, organized around a special sympathy for kin and friends: the first person I save from a burning shelter is my child or spouse, no deliberation needed. The second is a joint morality of collaboration in which I have specific responsibilities to specific individuals in specific cir-cumstances: the next person I save is the firefighting partner with whom I am currently collaborating (and with whom I have a joint commitment) to extinguish the fire. The third is a more impersonal collective morality of cultural norms and institu-tions in which all members of the cultural group are equally valuable.... The coexistence of these different moralities...is, of course, anything but peaceful (Tomasello, *Natural History*, p. 15).

The obsessional who embraces the unconstrained vision argues for the equality of all men, and that no one should be disadvantaged in a moral society.[24] But it is far different to be "endowed by one's Creator with certain inalienable rights," as the Preamble to the Declaration of Independence asserts, than to claim that all men are *literally* equal. Neither Thomas Jefferson, who authored the Preamble, nor the other Founding Fathers believed in the *literal* equality of men. They were well acquainted with the differences in human capacities and they founded America with that understanding. Progressives who argue for an egalitarian society are laboring under an illusion that shares no basis in experience, scientific observation, or common sense.

As Gelernter suggests, the American creed is based on decency and respect for the differences of its citizenry (Gelernter, 2007). While

---

24 In *Illiberal Education*, D'Souza notes that, at one West Coast university, a liberal Progressive professor argued that janitors should earn equal pay to the professors but never considered that the professors should earn equal pay to the janitors! (D'Souza, 1991)

imperfect, America is not a racist, bigoted, war-mongering nation that abuses minorities and the disadvantaged, as some Progressives suggest. All things considered, it is an honorable country that has done more to foster liberty in the world than any other nation in history. Yet what ought to be regarded as positive national character has been targeted by those who openly profess hatred for America. The glib comment by Governor Andrew Cuomo that "America has never been great," reflects either profound ignorance or purposeful distortion of the historical record.

As David Horowitz argues in *Unholy Alliance*, some Progressives exhibit greater sympathy for Islamic terrorists than for innocent American victims of terror. The Reverend Jeremiah Wright, the spiritual leader of the Trinity United Church of Christ that Barack Obama attended for many years in Chicago,[25] remarked, following the American tragedy of 9/11/2001, that "Terrorism begets terrorism," and then proceeded to quote the anti-American, anti-Semitic Black Muslim leader Elijah Muhammed by proclaiming that "America's chickens are coming home to roost." Rather than "God bless America, it should be God Damn America," preached Wright from the pulpit. For reasons driven by envy, hate, and anger, radical black "religious" leaders like Wright see America and its innocent citizens as legitimate targets for hateful violence. Such stances run counter to the natural bond of kinship in a society which, as Tomasello argues, is the core feature of morality.

Deep-seated hostilities can emerge when moralities are not shared.

---

25 One of the extraordinary facts of the 2008 presidential election was that Barack Obama, a veritable unknown on the national stage, was elected president with virtually no critical vetting. His relationship to the Reverend Wright, terrorists, and other members of the radical left might have given most Americans pause. But the liberal Progressive press failed to explore these facts in depth, apparently charmed by the notion of having the first African-American president. They adopted the same attitude to Obama throughout his two terms; he was rarely held seriously responsible for a series of fiascos and untruths.

This is known from the history of religion. Religionists develop affiliative bonds with those who share their morality, the so-called "in-group." The in-group may exhibit limited tolerance for those outside the group, but only if their values are not too disparate. For example, as an Abrahamic monotheistic religion, Islam shares a heritage with Judaism and Christianity that it does not with pagan religions, e.g., Buddhism[26] or Hinduism. For centuries, Jews and Christians living in the Islamic world were accepted as underclass minorities, whereas pagans were forced either to convert to Islam or die by the sword. But currently, even this degree of tolerance no longer exists in the eyes of Islamic fundamentalists. Islamic anti-Semitism has increased dramatically since the founding of the state of Israel, leading to expulsion of Jews from the Arab world, which they had traditionally called home for centuries. Coptic Christians are regularly killed in Egypt, and the Christian populations of Lebanon and Syria live in constant fear of violence (Horowitz, 2004). Yet these situations evoke little vocal concern by Progressives who espouse tolerance and diversity.

PROGRESSIVISM IS RELIGION

Progressivism is an ideology with professed origins in Christian values and, despite its secularity, it continues to espouse them. But in recent years it has adopted an extreme interpretation of Christian social justice. The Progressive agenda is currently focused on feminism, identity politics, and socioeconomic disparities, virtually to the exclusion of all other concerns.

Samuel Huntington argued poignantly in *Who We Are* that America's exceptional success on the world stage was primarily the result of the

---

26 The destruction of priceless ancient Buddhist statuary in *Bamiyan* by the Taliban is an example of how fundamentalist Islamists view paganism. Buddhism is an a-theistic tradition derived from pagan Hinduism, and therefore falls well beyond the pale for Islam.

efforts of the white European Protestants who founded the American colonies (Huntington, 2005). Prior to the 1960s, America absorbed millions of immigrants from all over the world, but the success of the immigrants depended on their willingness to adopt core American values and the English language. Assimilation was the goal and, whereas America has never been a "melting pot," new immigrants eventually assumed the values of their neighbors. But, since the mid-1960s, large scale migrations from Central America, Asia, the Middle East, and Africa, have brought immigrants to these shores who are unacquainted with and, in some cases, intolerant of, American values. Huntington argued that, if the assimilation of new immigrants is unsuccessful, American "exceptionalism" would be lost in the future.

Although widely viewed by Progressives as racist and bigoted, Huntington's ideas are neither; they are common sense confirmed by numerous sociological studies (C. Murray, 1984). Many Hispanics who come to this country illegally through the Southern border lack the educational preparation necessary to foster their integration into American society. Many are illiterate; they can neither read, write, nor speak the minimal amount of English required to gain employment and succeed in American society. Unfortunately, this trend in functional illiteracy now extends to native Americans as well, in large measure due to the failures of Progressive public education.

The success of a democratic republic requires a level of civic knowledge concerning its values and workings. It is questionable whether immigrants or many native-born citizens currently have the minimum education required to sustain a democracy (D'Souza, 1991). In the *Bell Curve* (Herrnstein & Murray, 1994), a controversial text, but one supported by abundant and compelling statistics, the authors suggest that the *mean* intelligence quotient (IQ) of African blacks and Mexican Hispanics on *average* is well below that of immigrants of

European descent. This does not suggest that people of color cannot be highly intelligent, but it does indicate genuine differences in intelligence on average that cannot be dismissed purely on the bases of ethnic, cultural, or socioeconomic backgrounds (C. Murray, 2020). Asians who have immigrated to America from very different cultures than our own routinely score high on these standardized tests, particularly in math and science, and rival or surpass native-born white Americans with respect to academic achievement.

These findings suggest that Progressive solutions to educational deficiencies are not likely to be effective, and historically they have not been (D'Souza, 1991). There is no credible evidence to suggest that differences in IQ scores and academic performance are lessened by socioeconomic entitlement programs or government-driven educational programs that cater to poor school performance. Other factors such as the high divorce rate, the absence of two parents in a household, and poor attitudes toward academic success are realities in many urban neighborhoods inhabited by people of color and may be factors in poor educational performance (C. Murray, 1999). But they are not addressed by Progressive programs for reasons of political correctness and because it challenges the Progressive mantra that all issues can be solved by the federal government by infusions of cash. Indeed, it is an obsessional trait to seek superficial strategies to "fix" situations rather than to confront unpleasant truths that require complex solutions.

IQ is the most accurate indicator of future socioeconomic success in American society. The findings noted above raise legitimate questions as to whether America would benefit in the future from being more selective in deciding who is permitted to immigrate if it is to maintain its status on the world stage (Herrnstein & Murray, 1994). When Progressives choose to dismiss this question as mean-spirited or "bigoted" and "racist," there is no possibility of entertaining real solutions. Progressivism claims to be rooted in "science"; that may have been the case in the past, but it is no longer. Rather than claiming to be "scientific" in its positions, its adherents should be forced to produce *credible* evidence to support them. Important questions deserve intelligent debate; they won't be solved by bandying about denigrating labels. As the adage goes, "If all you have is a hammer, everything looks like a nail," applies to the Progressive agenda of increased government spending as the cure for all ills.

Immigrants who arrive here illegally and are unable to speak English by necessity must live in ethnic communities to survive. Had they immigrated legally, they would have been given the education to foster citizenship. Without it, they are unlikely to achieve financial independence and must remain on the welfare rolls of the state or in low-paying jobs. The argument that they are needed to do jobs that American citizens won't do serves only to denigrate these immigrants as an established underclass. Opening our borders to illegal aliens is not compassionate; it is cruel.

Some, but certainly not all, legal immigrants from the Islamic world do not share the secular values of America. Their interpretation of Islam is antithetical to the secular values of feminism, gay rights, etc. They live in ethnic neighborhoods where they are confronted daily with having to choose between their newly adopted country and allegiance to the orthodoxies of their faith. However, conflict between secular and traditional religious values has not been problematic for all faiths, and this says something specific concerning the theocratic underpinnings of Islam. There are, for example, ultra-orthodox Jews, Christian Amish, and Mormons who choose to live as enclaves apart from the mainstream of secular American society, but they rarely have perpetrated terrorist attacks aimed at killing Americans.

The concept of *jihad*, or struggle, has two implications in Islam. It is both an individual struggle against moral imperfections, and a theocratic political struggle against the non-Islamic world. Progressives choose to ignore the latter, but it has been a core element of orthodox Islam since its inception. One need only read the Koran to identify the verse, "Slay the infidels wherever you find them!"

Whereas most Muslims do not participate in this militaristic element of their religion, most of these have been secularized, or have adopted a distinct liberal interpretation orthodoxy. But this may explain why open condemnation of fundamentalist terrorism by Muslims has been faint. In an interview in April 2019, the radical Progressive Islamic congresswoman from Minnesota, Rep. Ilhan Omar, summed up the 9/11 attack on America by Islamic terrorists by saying that it was not a terrorist attack on the U.S., but rather that, "Some people did something."

Boundaries are important both individually and in societies. This must be a consideration with respect to immigration if we are to maintain security and national integrity. "Extreme vetting," as Donald Trump puts it, is not bigotry; it's common sense, something distinctly lacking on the part of obsessional Progressives who prefer to maintain an unsupported optimism that things will eventually change for the better, or choose to accept an unnecessary increase in terrorist acts as the new normal, as much of Western Europe has.

Fundamentalist Islamic terrorism will not go away on its own. There is no appeasement, as British Prime Minister Neville Chamberlain learned after acceding to Hitler's demands in 1936, that will stop those who seek to destroy you, except to keep them at a distance or to destroy them first. Terrorists have no desire to share in the secular humanist "progress" of the West; those values hold no appeal for them. Therefore, it is the better part of wisdom to exclude foreigners from those Islamic countries where terrorism is rife unless one can be assured that their immigrating will ultimately benefit America. It is simply wrong-minded to do otherwise.[27]

SANCTUARY CITIES

Sanctuary cities have become fashionable among Progressives. Today there are cities, towns, and even states in America, all clamoring to be sanctuaries for illegal immigrants. The concept of a sanctuary city was adopted from the Hebrew Bible, and it is worthwhile to consider how the term was understood in its ancient context. A sanctuary city was an officially designated place where a man who had *accidentally* caused the death of another — what we might term involuntary manslaughter today — could flee from the vigilante retributive justice of the victim's family. But, if the killing was intentional, or if it was committed in the context of a crime, "sanctuary" was not granted. Instead, the guilty individual was to be promptly delivered to the nearest court, irrespective of his or her location, and removed even if still "holding to the horns of the altar," to be duly tried and, if found guilty, appropriately punished.

Contrast this with the notion of sanctuary in the Roman Catholic Church. Church Canon law suggests that sanctuary applies to *all* who seek it. Indeed, it was judged to be overly punitive to "imprison" fugitives within the confines of a church and they were allowed to wander freely within a specified distance (Shoemaker, 2011). Here again one encounters the alignment of the constrained vision with the teachings of Judaism and the unconstrained vision with the early Church. But, in America, where Progressivism has infected virtually all religions and denominations, one regularly hears calls for compassionate treatment

---

27 The difference between traditional Judaism and Christianity is worth noting here. Judaism explicitly allows one to defend oneself, even to the point of killing another who is pursuing you with murderous intent. Christianity emphasizes the need to "Love thine enemy." The former values survival; the latter is unconcerned with death.

and sanctuary for known criminals. A similar statement can be made for the Marxist terrorist group, Black Lives Matter, whose primary concern is not "black lives," as too many naïve Progressive white enthusiasts would like to believe, but the overthrow of the American political system.

Several Progressive American mayors and governors have been vocal in vowing not to deliver illegal immigrants, including those who have committed serious crimes, to the federal justice system for deportation, an idea without precedent in American history. If there is to be "one law" for citizens and resident aliens, then *both* must be subject to the *same* law. Illegal aliens have no legal rights under the Constitution, except to be treated humanely. Whereas Progressives argue that deporting illegal aliens is inhumane, there is little basis for that conclusion. There is no obligation, legal or moral, for a sovereign state to accept alien refugees, and there have been several examples in modern times of refugees seeking asylum for valid reasons having been denied.

There is no moral compulsion to establish open borders in a situation where certain immigrants may constitute a genuine danger to American citizenry, no matter how small the risk. Borders define the physical features of a nation; they are not provisional, and no nation can exist as such without them. Furthermore, lower court decisions to block the federal government's proposed temporary ban on immigration from a limited number of failed states represents an intrusion on the proper role of the Executive branch, especially when these Progressive jurists claim to know the real "racist" motivations for these orders. These lower court rulings are inevitably overturned by the U.S. Supreme Court when the cases are reheard because the president has the legal right to limit immigration. As for what is morally right, that is a matter of opinion. But in a nation of laws, opinions do not trump law.

There is little doubt that law can be morally unjust, but there are procedures in America that must be followed if they are to be changed. In the 1858 Supreme Court Dred Scott decision, slaves were judged not to have rights and could be returned to their "legal" masters as chattel. This decision was wrong but it held to the letter of the prevailing law of the time. It took a bloody civil war and an Executive Order — Lincoln's 1862 Emancipation Proclamation — to abolish slavery. But the problem of antebellum slavery in America should not be compared to the current problem of illegal aliens. Slavery was virtually ubiquitous in the ancient world. The slave trade was a part of early American history that has produced ongoing problems in America for 300 years. But the African slave trade brought people to America and enslaved them against their will. Most slaves were sold into slavery by black African chieftains for profit. Slavery was abolished 150 years ago, and progress in civil rights and race relations, while slow, has occurred rapidly over the last 60 years. Genuine progress would suggest that it is time to move on, but obsessional Progressivism refuses to do so, as it is stuck in the psychological realm of ancient grudges.

For those who share the constrained vision, the answer to illegal immigration is simple. Aliens actively transgress the laws of this country when they enter illegally. They are unvetted with respect to their previous lives; they may include an uncertain percentage of individuals with criminal histories, as well as some who harbor communicable diseases. Immigrants from failed states in the Middle East have no formal government of origin that can ensure vetting, and some may have terrorist designs.

Policies of open borders and sanctuary cities obstruct federal law, foster anarchy, and are a documented source of danger to law-abiding citizens. Those who are here illegally have already broken American law, which by itself defies the notion of good citizenship. It insults legal immigrants who spent years and money in their efforts to become citizens. Ultimately, in America there must be one law for all. It may be legitimate to ask what can be done for law-abiding illegal immigrants who were brought here as children; granting them citizenship would be an act of compassion on the part of the federal government, as it is under no legal or moral imperative to do so.

PROGRESSIVE GUILT

Conservative politicians argue that Progressivism is the cynical ideological underpinning for a political strategy designed to produce a dedicated voting bloc for future elections, by creating a welfare system for poor and undocumented citizens. Lyndon Johnson, who promoted the legislation of the Great Society in the 1960s, was a practiced politician. He viewed the social welfare policies directed at supporting the poor, blacks, and immigrant Hispanics as insurance for future Democratic party victories.

History has, for the most part, proved his strategy effective.[28] But not all Progressives are cynical politicians or positioned to strategize with respect to the results of future elections; as such, their motives must be sought elsewhere. In these cases, they can often be found in obsessionals who, like Kant, claim to embrace the unconstrained categorical imperative.

From a psychodynamic perspective, as Freud noted, the obsessional exhibits a harsh superego directed at failures to achieve childlike notions of perfection. These individuals were often as children held to unattainable standards by obsessional parents. They have learned to

---

28 The most recent example of this strategy proved unsuccessful for Hillary Clinton. Her strategy was clearly to carry the Obama coalition of blacks, Hispanics, and the poor. Unfortunately for her, she consistently ignored disaffected white voters in critical swing states.

feel guilty about having unacceptable thoughts and feelings and for not meeting the expectations of parents, teachers, and peers. Those who are to some degree "successful" continue to live in fear of failing in the future, and of losing the approval of others. This is not normal maturation.

It is difficult to distinguish primitive guilt from shame. Guilt generally refers to self-recriminations concerning transgressions toward others, whereas shame is a distressing affect that relates to having one's flaws exposed with the loss of self-esteem. Narcissists are famously subject to shame but rarely experience genuine guilt. Today's obsessionals suffer from both. They are hypersensitive about "harming" others, while scrupulously avoiding the critical scrutiny of others. The most glaring example today of Progressive guilt is what Shelby Steele has termed "white guilt," in which whites are manipulated into feeling unnecessarily guilty about the past abuses of slavery and the mistreatment of Native Americans. They are taught that America was stolen from the "Indians" and that our civilization achieved its success on the backs of slaves.

Although there is some truth in these claims, it is far from an accurate description of American success. But opportunistic Democratic politicians and racist black activists have tapped into the obsessional propensity to feel guilty without cause. In truth, no one alive in America today owns slaves. Indeed, most have ancestors who came to America well after slavery was abolished. There are few overt racists, and there is absolutely no credible evidence to support hyperbolic claims of "systemic racism," despite Progressive propaganda to the contrary (Mac Donald, 2016). Ezekiel 18:20 suggests that only someone who has committed a wrong himself is guilty and accountable: "The one who sins is the one who will die. The child will not share the guilt of the parent, nor will the parent share the guilt of the child. The righteousness of the righteous will be credited to them, and the wickedness of the wicked will be charged against them."

Obsessionals characteristically exhibit a defense mechanism termed "reaction formation." This was described by Freud and was summarized as follows by Calvin Hall (Hall, 1999):

[t]he instincts and their derivatives may be arranged as pairs of opposites: life versus death, construction versus destruction, action versus passivity, dominance versus submission, and so forth. When one of the instincts produces anxiety by exerting pressure on the ego either directly or by way of the superego, the ego may try to sidetrack the offending impulse by concentrating upon its opposite. For example, if feelings of hate towards another person make one anxious, the ego can facilitate the flow of love to conceal the hostility (Hall, *Primer*, p. 16).

This means the behavior of obsessionals often is the opposite of their true feelings. The fear of harming others under analytical scrutiny virtually always reveals covert hostility and a wish to do harm. The extraordinary lengths that obsessional Progressives go to to support those groups that they perceive as disenfranchised, in truth, belies their contempt toward them as inferior. As psychoanalyst Wilhelm Reich recognized, one invariably errs in taking the obsessional's "niceties" at face value (Reich, 1962). And the evidence for the reaction formations of obsessional Progressives is clear to the trained observer. What conclusions can be drawn concerning the true feelings of those who applaud free speech but then deny it to others on college campuses? Or exalt behaving politely and then going to the streets to destroy the property of others? Or those that decry the unwillingness of Donald Trump to unreservedly accept the results of an election, and then persist in protesting his unpredicted election as illegitimate for four years?

Actions speak louder and far more clearly than the words of obsessional Progressives.[29]

CONSCIENCE OF AN OBSESSIONAL

As Fromm argued, the obsessional has an uncomfortable and ambivalent relationship with rules and laws. Keenly aware of the expectations of others, he will adhere strictly to rules that others accept. However, should societal expectations change, he may be expected to undergo an extreme public shift in attitude. In a political climate where misogyny, bigotry, and racism are vehemently attacked as unacceptable, obsessionals who once expressed these positions will deny ever having held such views. Democratic presidential candidate Joe Biden is an excellent example of this. Biden's positions have shifted with the cultural tide many times over his 40-plus years in politics. In truth, he has no genuine convictions on any matter.

Despite their preoccupation with social justice, the conscience of obsessionals is defective and psychologically not integrated. Rather, it persists as an external "voice," one that since childhood has whispered into their ears what *should* be done, like Jiminy Cricket in the Walt Disney cartoon *Pinocchio*. Rules are followed carefully by obsessionals when they think they are being observed, as they fear that transgressions might be discovered and punished. When queried in analysis as to how they *really* feel about rules, obsessionals often exhibit a distinct lacuna in genuine conscience. In the extreme, this can manifest as sociopathy.

---

29 I reside in a liberal Progressive town in Massachusetts. It is a bastion of Progressive ideology inhabited by large numbers of Harvard professors. The churches in the town are draped with banners proclaiming that "Black Lives Matter." However, the affluent suburb includes virtually no African-American residents. The town has raised the idea of becoming a sanctuary for illegal aliens, but no one who is not affluent can possibly afford to live in the town. Furthermore, the presence of blacks is viewed with suspicion and can result in inquiries as to the nature of their business in town. What is the truth here? It is simply that ideas matter, not realities. The two rarely coincide in places like this across liberal Progressive America.

J. was a 36-year-old businessman who was raised in a fundamentalist Seventh Day Adventist family. While he was aware
of what was "moral," he admitted to never understanding what
the rules were about. When he came to analysis, he was having
an affair and afraid of being caught out, and concerned with
what others would think of him. However, he had no desire to
end the affair, which was mostly based on pure sexual attraction. He would repeatedly tell me that he knew he was "a bad
person" and promise to end his affair, but it was evident that
he had no intention of doing so. He was unable to experience
genuine guilt and had sociopathic tendencies in other areas as
well, including his business dealings.

Psychoanalyst Otto Kernberg has suggested that narcissistic individuals invariably exhibit a sector of sociopathy due to their grandiosity
and sense of entitlement (Kernberg, 1995). But what I am describing
here may have a distinct etiology. The conscience of the obsessional
is defective. Covert and hostile resistance to moral tenets force-fed
in an authoritarian home or strict religious environment contribute to
this moral lacuna, especially if they were construed by the child as
hypocritical.[30] The patient described above reported that many in his
fundamentalist religious community regularly transgressed the strict
rules of their religious sect when "no one was watching."

Obsessionals slavishly attend to bureaucratic regulations and are
highly critical of those who ignore them. Why then are obsessional
Progressives willing to disobey the law? The answer is two-fold. First,
because of their vulnerability to criticism, obsessional Progressives
support "political correctness" that allows zero tolerance for criticism

---

30 One of the unfortunate features of traditional religions has been the failure to communicate the benefits of religious practice to congregants. In the absence of meaningful communication of these benefits, it can be expected that secularism will replace them.

of those in society they judge to be vulnerable. This moral imperative allows them to skirt the law with impunity.

Obsessional Progressives perceive themselves as being watched and evaluated by others. They are pressured by parents, teachers, the media, and their peers to behave "correctly." While sensitive and compliant to what is expected of them, few question whether their own ideas or actions are authentic. They are prone to participate in a herd mentality, unwilling to stand apart with ideas that might invite criticism from others. This means they are left with the choice of either breaking the law, with the understanding that punitive responses are unlikely in the current political climate, or disappointing their Progressive peers. Those who do have ideas that run contrary to the herd will elect not to voice them in public.

In Nazi Germany, rules were carefully followed and immoral acts routinely carried out by the German people for fear of being shunned or worse by their neighbors and the regime. They were taught that ridding Germany of its Jews was a moral imperative, having been brainwashed by Nazi propaganda and centuries of European anti-Semitism. Hannah Arendt described the compliant immoral behavior of the German people as the "banality of evil." The herd mentality of obsessional Progressives is not, psychologically speaking, very different than that of the German people under the Third Reich. This should concern all Americans.

But, despite the diminished weight that Progressives place on laws that compromise their moral position, they are positively inclined to create new rules and regulations aimed at controlling the behavior of others. The Obama administration imposed more regulations on the financial and private sectors than any previous administration that was not actively engaged in a declared war with another nation state. This proclivity applies to virtually all levels of Progressive institutions.

Picayune regulations are enforced, at times with substantial punitive consequences for those who transgress them. Bureaucratic uniformity is fostered by new digital technologies that allow for wide-scale monitoring of the activities of others. Productivity is constantly measured, with new higher goals set on a regular basis, encouraged by minimal incentives. Progressivism is preoccupied with controlling the lives of others and, with the help of technology, it currently flirts with totalitarianism.

Like most obsessional concerns, the Progressive political agenda tends to miss the forest for the trees. Pressing existential issues of national concern are ignored, while social justice issues are minutely attended to. America faces real political and potentially military challenges from China, Iran, and North Korea. Progressive policies in the Middle East and Afghanistan left them in shambles and as a training ground for terrorists. The Progressive health care system, Obamacare, is financially untenable. Americans are unemployed, the economy is still underperforming due to the coronavirus, and the country is more than 20 trillion dollars in debt. These are real and existential challenges for America that must be confronted. Instead, Progressives are preoccupied with Donald Trump's tax returns, imagined examples of racism and misogyny, and absurd claims that Russia decisively interfered with the last election.

THE OBSESSIONAL ELITE

Economic advantages accrue to the obsessional elite. A cottage industry of institutional bureaucrats, charged with regulating behavior, promoting efficiency, and promulgating the political correctness agenda, has sprouted up over the last several decades. They are paid hefty salaries and occupy large offices. In turn, obsessional employees in these institutions are eager to carry out the new regulations efficiently, even when they serve to reduce their own freedom. Fromm termed this the "escape from freedom" that characterizes the obsessional personality (Fromm, 1960).

On the other side of the political spectrum, the obsessional whose conscience is rooted in the constrained vision is likely to believe that it is wrong to transgress established law under virtually any circumstance. These individuals are politically conservative, tend to vote with the Republican or Libertarian Parties, but find it impossible to support Donald Trump for personal reasons.

HYPOCRISY

It is easy to maintain one's opinion of oneself as a "good" person when one's true character is kept at bay. Psychologist Dan Ariely has made a career out of studying the factors that enhance dishonesty (Ariely, 2012). His findings echo the conclusion of Psalm 116:11 that, "All men are liars," although the degree to which individuals act deceitfully varies greatly.

A genuinely religious man who commits a "sin" will feel guilty about his transgression. Although he may initially choose to hide it, eventually he will confess it. Contrast this level of honesty with the Hollywood starlet who claims that "black lives matter," that illegal alien criminals deserve sanctuary, or protests against combatting global warming. Knowing virtually nothing about poor blacks or illegal aliens, and apparently unconcerned about global warming as she jets around the world increasing her carbon footprint, her words do little to help with her professed concerns. It is her distance from these situations that allow her to continue to believe that her morality is genuine. Is she disingenuous? Yes, to the extent that she believes she is telling the truth when she claims to be concerned with these issues. Is she a hypocrite? Perhaps, but to put it more generously — and likely accurately — she is accomplished at maintaining the illusion that she is telling the truth, precisely because she is sufficiently removed from the realities that she professes concern for. It should not be ignored that many in Hollywood are actors, and that the psychological complexity of their profession adds a layer of concern about truth telling that others may not experience. Suffice it to say, their qualifications in the political realm are limited, and they are generally not qualified to express expert opinions on such matters.

ALLEVIATING GUILT

For some obsessionals, the burden of moral perfectionism is too great to bear. The deleterious role of an overly harsh superego was addressed by Freud in the *Ego and the Id* (S. Freud, 1923). He sought to modify the harshness of the superego by determining the unconscious factors that motivate it. Freud never compromised on morality, but he did attempt to distinguish neurotic guilt from real culpability and to alleviate the suffering of those reacting to harsh internalized rules.

Freud's younger colleague, Sandor Ferenczi, espoused the opinion that any expression of superego in psychoanalysis should be expunged, in both the patient and the analyst (Ferenczi, 1955). According to Ferenczi, neither guilt nor judgment should guide the analytical treatment. This idea achieved an increasing degree of popularity in the British schools of psychoanalysis, and it is currently widespread in the helping professions.

As I suggested in *Parting of the Ways*, Freud adopted much of the metapsychology of psychoanalysis from the interdictions of Judaism (R. Kradin, 2016). The psychanalytical session is constrained by transactional boundaries and a variety of rules that apply to the conduct of both the analyst and patient and safeguard the treatment. When psychoanalysis entered the Christian world, elements of the unconstrained vision began to emerge. The concern for how this might transform psychoanalysis was noted by Heinz Kohut, the founder of self-psychology, itself a liberal modification of Freud's theory. According to Kohut's biographer (Strozier, 2001):

> Kohut felt the goal for revitalizing psychoanalysis was to get the Jews and Protestants to work together. The Jewish medical dominance of psychoanalysis in contemporary America was unfortunate, but if the institutes were dominated by Protestants alone (Kohut thought) it would probably move psychoanalysis toward non-scientific "healing through love"...which he saw as unfortunate (Strozier, *Making*, p. 136).

Psychoanalytic treatments informed by the unconstrained vision tend to emphasize empathy, compassion, forgiveness, love, etc. which, although therapeutic, systematically ignore the "dark" aspects of human nature, including anger, envy, jealousy, and selfishness, preferring to see them as aberrations that result from having been unsupported, treated punitively, or inadequately loved in childhood, rather than as the inheritance of man's animal nature.

There is little evidence to support the sustained therapeutic efficacy of pure empathy. Certainly, ill treatment at any stage of life can evoke pain and leave psychological scars, but it flies in the face of both science and history to conclude that man is innately pure at heart and no clear-eyed parent would agree with that conclusion. When the unconstrained view permeates society, truth suffers.

Striking examples of the exaggerated empathy of Progressives has been their unwillingness to prosecute criminals. While there is undoubtedly a political aspect to this, it is also a reflection of an inability to set limits. The current mayor of Seattle did nothing when "Black Lives Matter" militants seized six downtown blocks of her city. Instead, she ordered the police to step down and leave the scene. When questioned, she referred to what was taking place as a potential "summer of love." That is until several young blacks were killed and a terrorist mob descended on her own neighborhood, when she promptly ordered the downtown area cleared by the police. The mayor is an example of how excessive empathy and distance from unpleasant reality that character-izes so many Progressive elites endangers others.

MORAL MASOCHISM

Americans will undoubtedly see what results from enabling bad behavior. But why would Progressives choose a path of self-destruc-tion? Psychoanalysts have long recognized that obsessionals harbor covert feelings of moral grandiosity and choose to suffer rather than yield to what they perceive as injustice. In the *Economic Problem of Masochism* (S. Freud, 1924), Freud referred to this as "moral masoch-ism," and suggested that it was the reason why some people refuse to make progress in analysis. In such cases, there was a long-standing grudge concerning having been treated unfairly as a child by a parent:

The satisfaction of this unconscious sense of guilt is perhaps the most powerful bastion in the subject's (usually composite) gain from illness — in the sum of forces which struggle against his recovery and refuse to surrender his state of illness. The suffering entailed by neuroses is precisely the factor that makes them valuable to the masochistic trend. It is instructive, too, to find, contrary to all theory and expectation, that a neurosis which has defied every therapeutic effort may vanish if the subject becomes involved in the misery of an unhappy marriage, or loses all his money, or develops a dangerous organic disease. In such instances one form of suffering has been replaced by another; and we see that all that mattered was that it should be possible to maintain a certain amount of suffering (Freud, *Economics*, p. 166).

This psychological motif is exhibited by individuals and groups that feel powerless in the face of perceived mistreatment by powerful authority. The moral masochist may allow himself to be abused and even sacrificed if he can continue to imagine himself morally superior to authority.

This psychology is seen in Progressives who refuse to accept the authority of what they judge to be a morally imperfect America. This mindset is exemplified by the ancient Greek myth of Prometheus who, although chained to a mountain and tortured daily, refused to be released if it required acknowledging the authority of an unjust Zeus. This is the level of resistance that Progressives currently express toward Trump. This motif helps explain the otherwise inexplicable willingness of Progressive white academics to condemn the white race since, in so doing, they necessarily condemn themselves. It is, in part, based on the radical ideology of the early Church in which martyrdom was highly valued rather than submitting to pagan authority. But it also reflects a level of profound immaturity and grandiose perfectionism that, while normally outgrown, persists in the obsessional.

As Fromm suggested:

The different forms which masochistic strivings assume have one aim: *to get rid of the individual self, to lose oneself; in other words to get rid of the burden of freedom*.... If the individual finds cultural patterns that satisfy these masochistic strivings, he gains some security by finding himself united with millions of others who share these feelings (Fromm, p. 151-52).

President Trump is the embodiment of bankrupt morality for these perfectionistic masochists, who view themselves as morally superior to him and those millions of Americans who voted for him. They denied the legitimacy of his election in 2016, as they were "certain," albeit without evidence, that it could only have been stolen by immoral opponents. Through their grudging behavior, they chose to undermine the governance of the country rather than admit defeat. This behavior is reminiscent of how Homer described Achilles choosing to sit out the Trojan War in his tent because he was unjustly slighted by Agamemnon. Progressive politicians in America recapitulate the behavior of moral masochists and are properly termed pathological.

This psychological motif explains the Obama foreign policy of "leading from behind" and his famous apology tour in the Middle East, in which he confessed America's guilt for being a world leader. Based on his biography, Obama had reason for bearing a grudge with white America and with a father who abandoned him early in life. The refusal of Progressives, like Obama, to name and condemn radical Islamic terrorism while denigrating America is another symptom of masochism. Howard Schwartz suggested in his *Revolt of the Primitive* (Schwarz, 2003) that masochism is a core element of political correctness, which undermines success in government and in the private sector.

It is critical to recognize that the stances adopted by Progressives are not moral; rather, they are self-defeating positions driven by childish perfectionism, envy, hate, and an intractable grudge with America-as-a-bad-parent. Their actions will succeed in driving America down if allowed to continue. But what transpired in America since the 1960s to foster this self-defeating stance?

CHAPTER 5: EXISTENTIAL INSECURITY

The idea of death haunts the human animal like nothing else;
it is a mainspring of human activity.

— Ernst Becker

In his treatise *Denial of Death,* Ernst Becker argues that the psychology of man is imbued with a compulsive need to deny his own mortality (Becker, 1973). Linking the notion of the heroic to man's narcissism, he suggests that society is a symbolic system, in which "statuses and roles, customs and rules for behavior" are all aimed at achieving imaginal immortality. In earlier times, these symbols were embedded in a matrix of religious ideas and rituals that served to construct meaning out of life. Whether immortality was fostered through the practice of good works or through grace, the survival of the soul was assured. Even those who did not merit salvation were relegated to some mode of experience in an afterlife. Therefore, an imaginal sentient element of "life" continued to survive death in an imaginal *topos*. These ideas served to buffer the individual from the nihilism of finitude.

With the emergence of science and secularism, traditional religious beliefs no longer sufficed to assure many that "life" survived the grave.

Although it is virtually impossible to imagine pure "absence," some secular individuals claim to prefer that to an afterlife that cannot be proved scientifically. But, when religious beliefs are challenged, so are the primary sources of meaning and morality. Whereas some scholars have argued for centuries that man is innately moral and that a coherent secular morality would have naturally emerged independent of religion, that conclusion is questionable. According to philosopher Irving Kristol (Kristol, 1995):

> The philosophical rationalism of secular humanism can at best provide us with a statement of the necessary assumptions of a moral code, but it cannot deliver on any such code itself. Moral codes evolve from the moral experience of communities and can claim authority over behavior only to the degree that individuals are reared to look respectfully, even reverently, on the moral traditions of their forefathers. It is the function of religion to instill such respect and reverence (Kristol, *Neoconservatism*, p. 450).

Morality, like other complex psychological expressions, has multiple determinants. It can reflect deep-seated reverence for the welfare of others or it can be false and neurotically driven. The main difference between obsessional actions and religious rituals for Freud was that the latter were imbued with meaning for the practitioner, whereas the actions of the obsessional neurotic represented frustrated efforts at construing meaning for a life ruled by anxiety and doubt (S. Freud, 1907).

In *Future of an Illusion*, Freud argued that the religious impulse resists uncontrollable events and the finitude of human life through magical thinking (S. Freud, 1927). Many have criticized Freud's view of religion, which he viewed simply as a persistent childhood need to identify with a powerful protective father. This mode of thinking was appropriate in a worldview dominated by magical thinking. But, Freud argued, religion must now be set aside in favor of reason and science: "The whole thing is so patently infantile, so foreign to reality, that to anyone with a friendly attitude to humanity, it is painful to think that the majority of mortals will never be able to rise above this view of life" (Freud, *Future*, p. 138). Freud's appreciation of religion lacks sophistication and, while it may apply to the religious beliefs of a simple man, it does not pertain to a trained theologian. Nevertheless, his recognition of the outward similarities of religious ritual and obsessional neurosis remain valid.

Freud's hopes for a culture based on secular humanism and devoid of religious belief have not been achieved. Despite his desire to expunge superstition from the societal *weltanschauung*, religion has merely been replaced by other obsessional systems, including Progressivism. This "ism" represents an ideology that views progress as the expression of rationality, science, technology, economic development, and social organization. For those who endorse it, it is the path toward "perfecting" the human condition.

The Hegelian notions of progress guided by spirit and the dialogical process of thesis, antithesis, and synthesis represent an approach in which the old paternalistic systems of the past are deconstructed in order to progress[31] (Hegel, 2016). Informed by Christian morality, Progressivism is rooted in a socialist moral agenda. But, in the eight years under Barack Obama's leadership, it adopted a more intense left-wing vision.

The Progressives of early 20th CE American politics were critical of the Calvinistic "individualism" of the Founding Fathers. Instead of a government that protects individual rights by limited, decentralized

---

31 The left-wing organization "Move on.org," financed in large part by multi-billionaire George Soros, has adopted this motto.

power, they envisioned an expansive central government, with a "living" and flexible Constitution, led by intellectual elites. The average individual would not have to engage in political decision making, and would instead be free to pursue his full potential in other areas, while a concerned government made decisions that would unburden him of responsibility. This idea in many respects parallels the thinking of the bureaucracy of the Roman Catholic Church, whose lay members often have little sophisticated understanding of their religion, as it is thought to be beyond their need to understand. The mysteries of the religion are left to an elite clergy.[32]

Karl Marx in his *Communist Manifesto* described religion in wholly negative terms (Marx & Engels, 2014). Religion, argued Marx, was the "opiate of the people"; its primary role was to foster exploitation by a wealthy ruling class. Whereas Marx's ideas did not take hold in the West, they formed the basis of the atheistic Soviet Union that collapsed in 1989, largely in response to an upsurge of religious fervor within the Eastern European bloc.

Despite its Christian roots and purported tolerance of religious freedoms, modern Progressives view institutional religion as a conservative anachronism and as an impairment to progress. For Hegel, it was the nation state, not the Church, that supported the "divine idea as it exists on earth" (Hegel, 2016). John Burgess, a prominent Progressive political scientist, argued that the purpose of the nation state is the "perfection of humanity, the civilization of the world; the perfect development of the human reason and its attainment to universal command over individualism; the *apotheosis of man*," i.e., man becoming God (Nugent,

---

32 It may not be entirely fair to single out the Roman Catholic Church for this behavior, as elements of it are seen in virtually all religious traditions today. Jewish rabbis, Protestant ministers, Muslim imams, and Buddhist monks all generally are far more knowledgeable concerning their traditions than laymen, but the system of the Roman Catholic Church was, for historical reasons, organized around a poorly educated lay public, who were encouraged to take their religion purely on faith.

2010). The stridency in positions adopted by some liberal Progressives cannot be viewed as anything less than Marxist-style "religious" intolerance.[33] Short of prohibiting religious practice, Progressivism calls for its reformation in terms that are acceptable to the Progressive agenda.

However, the unconscious religious motifs that motivate Progressives have remained essentially undisturbed. Rather than assuming the old forms of divinely directed contemplation and rituals, they manifest now as secular obsessional strategies. The re-emergence of religious motifs in secular Progressivism is a cardinal example of what Freud referred to as the "return of the repressed."

Freud argued, in *Civilization and Its Discontents*, that civilized society is a "substitute-formation" (S. Freud, 1933). But he continues to aver that this notion of novelty is mistaken. Instead, what is repressed as part of the socialization process tends to re-emerge, and this may include for some the belief in a transcendent Being. Progressivism reflects this repressed motif in its aim of centralizing control over others and participating in a new "creation." It is the re-emergence of religious ideation in secular guise. Obsessional neurosis is characterized by repetitive behaviors that result from repressed ideas and feelings that are unrecognized due to failures of insight. Until self-knowledge is achieved, one can expect obsessional strategies to recreate themselves as ideological "isms."[34]

---

33 In intercepted e-mail conversations of Clinton campaign manager John Podesta, one of the leaked conversations included the "backward" ways of the Catholic Church and how something needed to be done to overcome them.

34 Chasidic philosophy speaks of three levels of cognition. The first reflects the initial spar of a new idea (*Chochmah*). This is followed by the ability to discern and develop the idea (*Binah*). Finally, the idea needs to be integrated into the substance of the mind's repertoire (*Daath*). It is this last step that does not occur for the obsessional. As a result, the same ideas re-emerge both at the individual and societal levels. There is little real "progress" in Progressivism.

TRAUMA AND EXISTENTIAL INSECURITY

Trauma, both physical and psychological, enhances existential insecurity. What has been termed "stress" in the lay and psychotherapeutic literature is an ill-defined concept derived from the physical sciences, where it connotes the deformation of a material structure. The term was introduced into common parlance by Hans Selye, a physiologist studying the hormonal reactions of laboratory animals to varying insults in the 1950s (R.L. Kradin & Benson, 2000). Selye's findings proved to be a great advance in recognizing how the brain and neuroendocrine system react to physical and psychological disturbances.

Studies by Walter Cannon in the 1930s examined the behavioral reactions of animals to danger, and his findings have informed psychological theorists with respect to the behavioral reactions to traumatic stress (Cannon, 1932). Cannon appreciated that, when threatened, animals tend to "fight or flight." Subsequent observations demonstrated that animals also freeze in inaction, e.g., play 'possum, or alternatively seek affiliation with others who may be able to provide safety. As previously discussed, the primary strategy of the obsessional is to avoid stressful confrontations or to freeze in inactivity (Janet, 1921). But, at the collective level today, we recognize the tendency to affiliate as well, either on social media or in public demonstrations by like-minded obsessionals. The political party system in America also provides individuals with the opportunity to affiliate with like-minded people who can provide "security" in numbers.

21st CE America is a stressful place, although it may be less existentially dangerous than in the past, when populations were regularly ravaged by war and disease. In the post-war 1950s, one could imagine as Ronald Reagan's election advertisement suggested, that it was "morning in America" with wheat gently swaying in the breeze and families sitting in harmony together at the dinner table. Digital technologies have changed these tranquil images.

Today, those who have smart phones — and few do not — are constantly barraged by e-mails, text messages, and other alerts, all screaming for immediate attention. The idea of a Sabbath or a weekend undisturbed by the demands of the workplace are increasingly rare. America's security has been threatened by Islamic terrorists, a wave of violent crime in our inner cities, and the omnipresent background fear of purposeful or error-driven nuclear, biohazard, or power grid apocalypses. The ability to communicate streaming images of war and disaster widely through the media has left individuals with no escape unless they choose to "live off the grid."

America is technologically more advanced but less secure than ever. It should come as little surprise that, to distract themselves, many now spend considerable amounts of time playing video games, watching television, or visiting online pornography sites. Their engagement with virtual realities appears to have made it difficult for Americans to distinguish virtual reality from the real thing. As Umberto Eco argued in his monograph on *Travels in Hyperreality*, what is without flaws but not real may have more attraction for many perfectionists than the coarseness of the material world (Eco, 1990).

Following the cessation of hostilities in World War II, America lapsed into a false sense of invulnerability. It was jolted back to reality by a series of assassinations, including those of President John F. Kennedy, his brother Sen. Robert Kennedy, and civil rights leader Martin Luther King in the 1960s. This accompanied a long, unpopular, and ultimately unsuccessful war in Vietnam in the 1970s that was punctuated by civil disturbances and followed by the precipitous collapse of the Soviet Union in the late 1980s. In the late 1970s, the HIV epidemic left many people fearful for their physical lives and avoidant of sexual intimacy. These events contributed to a growing realization among complacent Americans that the world was no longer a predictable or safe place.

Until the Islamic terrorist attack of 9/11/2001, America had been physically isolated from destruction on its own soil. On that day, war came to America. This was followed by seemingly interminable threats of terrorism, wars in Iraq and Afghanistan — which, like the Vietnam War, have no clear end-game — and the gnawing recognition that government is incapable of fully protecting us from sudden trauma and death. For today's young men who have never had to face conscription into the Army, where traditionally "boys became men," and who have been overly protected from even the minor traumas of daily life, fears of hostility can evoke avoidance, denial, panic, or paranoid ideation. They are important contributors to the emergence of obsessionality.

A perceived loss of control and the emergence of chaotic affect triggers anxieties that signal the need to re-establish security, especially for the obsessional. One of Freud's great observations was that the conscious ego has specific and redundant defenses that protect it from experiencing overwhelming levels of anxiety. These mechanisms were explicated, based on the works of her father, by Anna Freud as *Defenses of the Ego* (A. Freud, 1962).

Persistent stress triggers intellectual rationalizations that can reduce discomfort temporarily. But, whether they are simple fantasies or complex ideologies, they are fictions based on magical thinking (S. Freud, 1936). In America today, many people live in an illusory bubble that threatens their ability to recognize and respond to real existential threats.

Cognitive distortion and limitation of experience are the *sine qua non* of neurosis. They isolate the ego from the perception of threat. In addition to internal ego defenses, factors external to the individual have also been recruited in the service of protecting the ego. The Internet today provides innumerable distractions and alternative "realities" so that fearful individuals can readily escape unpleasant realities. Walk down the halls of virtually any office in America and you are likely to find workers shopping, playing games online, or "surfing the net."

The ability to deny real existential threat is fostered by those post-modern academic scholars who refer to "reality" as a construct that may be interpreted in a variety of ways (Sowell, 2011). This mode of thinking has little practical value; it does not provide "a greater capacity to deal with ambiguity"; instead, it appeals to minds that prefer to retreat into a realm of virtual possibilities rather than to confront real threats.

Adopting Panglossian optimistic narratives in the face of danger is also a mode of neurotic avoidance that ultimately leads to disastrous results. A prime historical example was British Prime Minister Neville Chamberlain's policy of appeasement of Adolph Hitler's aggression in Europe. Chamberlain chose to ignore the clearly expressed aggressive plans of Hitler and instead optimistically chose to preserve the illusion of "Peace in our times." It took a World War, and a strong leader in Winston Churchill, to snatch Great Britain from the jaws of defeat. In America, Barack Obama's refusal to identify terrorist threats to the American homeland, his "deals" with the terrorist-supporting Iranian regime of mullahs, and his failure to address the serious nuclear challenges raised by a rogue state in North Korea, are all examples of effete, overly optimistic, and avoidant obsessional "rationales." Obama's dithering concerning critical decisions highlights the concerns that Americans should have when they choose to elect obsessionals as leaders. Obsessionals are not up to jobs that require decisive action and confrontation, no matter how charismatic, intelligent or articulate they may be.

Chapter 6: Language and the Myths of Obsessionality

In the beginning was the Word, And the Word was with God,
And the Word was God.

— Prologue to the 4th Gospel of John

Carl Jung opined that man's greatest challenge is to identify the myth that guides his experience (C.G. Jung & Jaffe, 1959). The same can be said of a society. The myth of obsessionality emerged with human consciousness and man's wish to control his environment.

Ancient creation myths emphasize how order was imposed upon unruly chthonic forces. In the Babylonian creation myth, the young male god *Marduk* slays the primitive female sea dragon *Tiamat* who had hitherto dominated the primordial universe (Levenson, 1994). *Marduk* divides *Tiamat* with his sword, thereby superimposing order on chaos. Tiamat's body is subsequently used to create the earth, reconfiguring it as an inhabitable and predictable domain for man to dwell in.

The creation myth of Genesis 1:1 alludes to the older Babylonian myth, in which the "spirit of God hovers over the watery depths (*tehom*)," *tehom* being the Hebrew cognate of *Tiamat*. Whereas the biblical creation is generally accepted as a *creatio ex nihilo*, a close reading of the text appears to suggest that the world was created out of a pre-existing watery world that was subsequently ordered by divine fiat.[35]

The power of cognition is suggested by Genesis 1:1, in which the world is created by ten divine utterances. The "Let there be.... and there was" motif suggests that the world was structured via Divine thought. In later Kabbalistic texts, such as *Sefer Yetzirah*, that dates to the 2-3rd CE, creation is attributed to innumerable permutations of the 10 cardinal numbers and the 22 letters of the Hebrew alphabet, suggesting that creation is the result of a complex intelligence. Indeed, the uniformity of physical laws that allows scientists to study and predict events anywhere in the universe suggests an intelligent set of structural rules.

The Christian re-conception of Genesis adopts the concept of the *Word*, or *logos* — first described by Philo, a Hellenized Jew of the 1st CE in Alexandria, or as *Memra* (word) in Aramaic *Targums*[36] — as the source of creation (R. Kradin, 2016). The *logos,* referred to in ancient Hebrew and Christian Gnostic texts as Wisdom, is referred to in the preamble of the Gospel of John as a hypostasis of God. The Word/Wisdom is imagined as having been present since the beginning of time, personified as a demiurge through which the material world was created. Much as man is the microcosm of Divine creation, language plays a role in the emergence of what we know as human consciousness. In the absence of self-reflective thought and speech, man differs little from other animals that are prone to instinctual sexuality and out-

---

35 This has been widely noted by biblical scholars, including Jon Levenson at Harvard Divinity School (Levenson, 1994), but the official monotheistic credo is a *creation ex nihilo*. This point was made by Maimonides in his *Guide for the Perplexed* in differing with the pagan Aristotelian notion of creation (Maimonides, 2000).

36 After the Babylonian Exile in the 6th BCE, many Jews were no longer literate in ancient Hebrew and required translations (*Targums*) into Aramaic, which was the *lingua franca* in much of the ancient Middle East.

bursts of aggression.[37] Thought and language are the essential psychological strategies for the containment of human instincts and emotions, much as they were mythically imagined to structure the chaos of the primordial universe. In civilized society, emotions are optimally meant to be conveyed by words, but that is still a substantial effort for many.

The neurotic obsessional "thinks too much." This is not an adage; it is a quantifiable fact. The mind of the obsessional is driven by increased cognitions (Association, 1994; Ingram & May, 1961). Verbal intelligence is also, on average, increased in obsessionals (Ingram & May, 1961), whereas emotional intelligence is reduced. Intellectuals include a high proportion of obsessionals, a fact with societal consequences.

The evolution of society and, more broadly, civilization, hinges on how language is used. The history of language demonstrates that words, originally signifiers of the material world, can be adopted to represent ideas removed from tangible reality. Language constructs a symbolic universe of ideas. These ideologies can be interesting but also misleading and dangerous.

As Hannah Arendt explains in *Origins of Totalitarianism* (Arendt, 1976):

An ideology is quite literally what its name indicates: it is the logic of an idea. Its subject matter is history, to which an "idea" is applied; the result of this application is not a body of statements about something that is, but the unfolding of a process which is in constant change.... Ideologies pretend to know the mysteries of the whole historical process — the secrets of the past, the intricacies of the present, the uncertainties of the

---

37 Judaism refers to four categories of earthly existence, inorganic matter (*domeh*), plant life (*tzomeh*), animal life (*chai*), and man who "speaks" (*medaber*), emphasizing the unique quality of human thought and speech.

future — because of the logic inherent in their respective ideas (Arendt, *Origins*, p. 176).

The problem with ideology is that ideas can be rational without applicability to the real world. Furthermore, ideologies are invariably overly simplistic because they are derived from a single or small number of core concepts that are then imposed on complex realities. As Arendt continues:

> The claim to total explanation promises to explain all historical happenings, the total explanation of the past, the total knowledge of the present, and the reliable prediction of the future. Secondly, in this capacity, ideological thinking becomes independent of all experience from which it cannot learn anything new even if it is a question of something that has just come to pass (Arendt, *Origins*, p. 203).

Ideologies are best interpreted as explanatory structures that serve to contain societal angst. Unfortunately, conclusions drawn from them may be incorrect. But once an ideology is entrenched, like a mathematical attractor, it resists alternative explanations.

While ideologies are mental "constructs" in biological terms, they reflect underlying specific patterns of neuronal activation in the brain that with repeated usage become increasingly resistant to change (Edelman, 1989). The obsessional responds to anxiety with ideological narratives. The obsessional individual does not consider the complexities of experience. Kant's categorical moral imperative is such an example. Rational, devoid of feeling, and unrelated to empirical experience, this quintessential obsessional philosopher called for a perfectionistic approach to morality, one far removed from normal daily life.

In the past, ideologies were developed by intellectuals and slowly disseminated by word of mouth or in books. Today, Progressive ideology is widely disseminated as propaganda via the mainstream news and social media, so that large segments of society have come to share simplistic beliefs that resist alternative explanations. Ideologies foster a herd mentality and "groupthink," and they are reinforced by fears of disapproval. In parts of America today, it is virtually impossible to oppose the ideology of Progressivism without fear of reprisals from friends, colleagues, and institutions. As Arendt suggests:

> The propaganda of the totalitarian movement also serves to emancipate thought from experience and reality; it always strives to inject a secret meaning into every public, tangible event and to suspect a secret intent behind every public political act (Arendt, *Origins*, p. 304).

Consider this description in light of the constant accusations of conspiracies in the new Trump administration, its racism, bigotry, etc. The politics of Progressivism in America today have grown uncomfortably close to totalitarianism. This should concern all Americans, regardless of their political affiliations.

KNOWLEDGE AND NEWS

We live in an age of information in which one encounters streams of data literally everywhere one turns. Social media has resulted in unprecedented information sharing, a role previously played primarily by the mainstream press. Currently, "news" can be introduced in real time and rapidly disseminated, with little or no critique concerning its veracity, by anyone with a smart phone with a camera.

The coverage of both the 2016 and 2020 presidential elections witnessed a near-complete breakdown in journalistic objectivity. Journalists on network news, as a rule part of the liberal Progressive elite, relentlessly introduced their own opinions, and chose to highlight, exaggerate, misquote, or suppress facts that did not support the Progressive ideology. They focused on vilifying President Trump's character and policies, and made a concerted effort to portray his election as illegitimate. Disturbingly, with little evidence, they then accused Conservative media sites of participating in the very activities they themselves were engaged in.

As most Americans unfortunately have neither the time nor the inclination to identify primary sources, these remarkably skewed journalistic portrayals have the potential to influence American politics based on fabricated facts. But it was not entirely lost on Americans that the mainstream media had lost touch with the truth, and polls have consistently shown that their favorability ratings have fallen to new lows.

According to Michael Snyder, who writes for the media news outlet www.activistpost.com:

> A recent survey conducted by a liberal polling firm found that only 6% of Americans consider MSNBC to be their most trusted source for news…. NBC News and sister cable network MSNBC rank at the bottom of media outlets Americans trust most for news, with Fox News leading the way, according to a new poll from the Democratic firm Public Policy Polling. In its fifth trust poll, 35% said they trusted Fox News more than any other outlet, followed by PBS at 14%, ABC at 11%, CNN at 10%, CBS at 9%, 6% for MSNBC and Comedy Central, and just 3% for NBC…

A recently released Pew Research study discovered that the decline of America's newspapers continued in 2013 as well…. It took a half-century for annual newspaper print ad revenue to gradually increase from $20 billion in 1950 (adjusted for inflation in 2013 dollars) to $65.8 billion in 2000, and then it took only 12 years to go from $65.8 billion in ad revenues back to less than $20 billion in 2012, before falling further to $17.3 billion last year (Pew Research, May 19, 2014).

This is objective evidence of how unpopular the mainstream media has become. But it also suggests that individuals may no longer be interested in mainstream journalism and prefer to get their news on social media (Goddfried & Shearer, 2016). The purveyors of these sites generally hold Progressive views, and fact-checking is not a routine aspect of their reporting. In the lead-up to the 2020 election, social media giants, including *Google*, *Facebook*, *Twitter*, and their off-shoots, all made concerted efforts to suppress negative stories about the Biden campaign and to censor President Trump, in an effort to influence the election; they evidently succeeded at the task. Such election interference is unprecedented in American history. Although, from a post-modernist scholar's perspective, it may be argued that "all truth is constructed," the late Senator Patrick Daniel Moynihan's statement still rings true, "Everyone is entitled to his own opinion, but not to his own facts."

Whereas complete objectivity may be difficult to achieve, the obsessional mind creates narratives that are invariably distorted. Neurotic rationalization functions specifically to create illusions and forms the basis for the ideological positions of the Progressive left, which are increasingly unsupported by empirical data. The dissemination of faulty ideas has become a staple of modern society and actively contributes to the widening schism between Americans.

The constant flow of verbal information favors cognition over other modes of experience. Whether one thinks too much as an ego-defense or as the result of the technological demands of a changing world, the result may be the same, i.e., an obsessional style characterized by excessive cognition and restricted affect.

There is little time in today's workplace for relaxed conversation. The driving motivation appears to be getting one's work done rapidly and efficiently. This abhorrence of "waste," be it time, money, or materials, is a recognized obsessional trait.

> A middle-aged married executive woman with obsessional character remarked that she was not allowed to "waste time" when growing up. Relaxation and sitting still were discouraged. She complained of wasting time at work. She spent large amounts of time on the weekends recycling to make sure that little was wasted. She rationalized this by insisting that it was good for the planet. She was uncomfortable with psychotherapy as it did not provide immediate results and she did not want to waste good time and money. Her goals were outer directed and constantly in flux.

Obsessionals in therapy are uncomfortable with the open-endedness of the process, preferring defined goals instead. They are unable to free-associate to their own ideas and feelings.[38] They adopt mechanical metaphors for the treatment, declaring that they want to "fix" themselves or make themselves "better." They do not wish to waste time or money, especially when success cannot be quantified. The concept of organic healing eludes them, as that implies that change can emerge naturally without their input.

---

38 Free-association was Freud's cardinal rule for psychoanalysis. It is rarely adopted in today's relational therapies. It included insisting that the patient's attempt to speak in an uncensored way concerning all thoughts and feelings that might arise while the analyst silently listened and occasionally opted to interpret what he was hearing.

SCHOLARSHIP

Prior to the Internet, a scholar was a well-read storehouse of information and ideas. Access to the Internet has changed this. Most young scholars do not spend large amounts of time reading texts. Many instead rely on the Internet to provide pre-digested information on websites like *Wikipedia,* which offer immediate access to a universe of superficial information but rarely provide a perspective that one can gain from reading an author's ideas on a subject in depth. Today's scholars argue that it is inefficient to store information in one's memory banks when it can be readily accessed online. But this attitude leads to a superficial understanding, knowledge sufficient to support a fancy PowerPoint presentation, but lacking what is required for expertise. Superficiality is compounded by a trend toward specialization, so that few currently have a broad grasp of their field.

There are few remaining polymaths. As Sowell notes, a professor of sociology today has little credibility when he comments on economics. One must wonder whether intellectuals espousing opinions on virtually any topic merit serious attention, even at times within their own area of "expertise." Consider the erroneous predictions of health experts, like Dr. Anthony Fauci, about how to address the coronavirus epidemic. Fauci has been a fixture at the NIH and Washington for decades. He does not care for patients, which is a full-time art in itself. Although he did interesting research on AIDS, he is not an infectious disease expert with specialized knowledge of respiratory viruses. We are currently confronting a genuinely novel infection in Covid-19. His guess — and it is at best a guess — about how best to address the pandemic is as good as mine, and I *do* have expertise in respiratory viruses, having authored textbooks on the topic. Yet, compelled by ego and responsibility, or perhaps both, Fauci, and others have made a series of erroneous statements that have mostly served to frighten an already beleaguered public. To his credit, Kentucky Sen. Rand Paul, a physician, recognized that the predictions made by Fauci and other health "experts" leave much to be desired and called him out on this in recent Senate investigations into the pandemic.

And, if this is true of trained scholars, to what extent is someone in the entertainment industry qualified to comment on politics? Unfortunately, American politics has increasingly become a popularity contest, with film and TV celebrities vying with each other for the nation's highest offices, and too often winning them.

KNOWLEDGE AS POWER

The popular adage that "knowledge is power" carries great weight for the elite obsessional. In Plato's *Republic,* Socrates argues that the city-state should ideally be ruled by philosophers, whose knowledge would facilitate the harmonious co-operation of its citizens (Bloom, 2016). The philosopher-king is the role model for elite society. But his merit is too often removed from the daily realities of the common man.

In the history of religion, Gnosticism, a 2nd CE Middle Platonic Christian philosophy, espoused the view that salvation could only be achieved by those with esoteric knowledge. The Gnostics divided mankind into the *pneumatikoi,* an intellectual elite that would ultimately be saved, the *psychikoi,* who with effort might merit salvation, and the fleshy *sarkikoi,* who were beyond all hope. Gnosticism led to a schism within early Christian society, and the Church Fathers rejected it as elitist, as it denied salvation to *all* who believed in the resurrection of Christ. As Paul warned in *Colossians* 2:8:

See to it that no one takes you captive through philosophy and empty deceit, according to human tradition, according to the elemental spirits of the universe and not according to Christ.

In medieval times, a resurgence of Gnosticism occurred among the Cathars of the Languedoc of Southern France (Sumption, 2000). The Cathars argued that only those with esoteric knowledge, the *perfecti*, were prepared to lead the community. This led Roman Pope Innocent III to call for the Albigensian crusade, in which this heretical sect was brutally eliminated.

The quest for power through knowledge is part of the myth of Progressivism, an ideology that recapitulates Gnosticism in its notion of an intellectual elite that is best positioned to lead. From their perspective, "fleshy" Conservatives will have no share in America's future.

CHAPTER 7: FEMINISM AND IDENTITY POLITICS

God may be in the detail, but the Goddess is in connection.

— Gloria Steinem

Where love reigns, there is no will to power; and where the will to power is paramount, love is lacking. The one is but the shadow of the other.

— C.G. Jung

WHAT DO WOMEN WANT?

Freud has never been popular among feminists. He famously once stated in a letter that, "The great question that has never been answered, and which I have not yet been able to answer, despite my thirty years of research into the feminine soul, is 'What does a woman want?' (Jones, 1953) The rise of the feminist movement has had a profound effect on America and on the direction of Progressivism. The women's movement has influenced our ideas concerning what is acceptable in society and transformed the aims of obsessionality, as well.

The aims of feminism have been a moving target. In her introduction to *Modern Feminist Theory*, Jennifer Rich refers to a conversation that she overheard at a women's discussion group, in which members of the group attempted to define what are the major goals of feminism (Rich, 2007):

(Some said the)… demand for equal rights, some that it involved the dismantling of the sex/gender system, still others that it was an unending struggle against male domination in all of its forms. Finally, an eight-year old girl who had been listening intently to the conversation asked the following: "Isn't feminism the belief that women are human beings?" (Rich, Intro, p. 1).

Although the young girl's question is worthy of an answer, substantial energy has been directed at defining women based on dismantling gender and opposing the power of men. Feminism has clearly made substantial inroads in the culture. There are few men in America today, even among those who do not view themselves as supporters of the feminist movement, who would not agree that women should be treated fairly, respected, and compensated equally to men.

In Freud's time, prior to the emergence of feminism, obsessionality was viewed as a male attribute, whereas the emotionality of women was linked to the hysterical style. Indeed, it was argued in Freud's time that male hysteria never occurred.[39]

Popular books like John Gray's *Men are from Mars, Women are from Venus* have addressed the differences in cognitive and relational styles between the sexes (Gray, 2012). But women have always exhibited obsessional styles, and my experience in psychoanalytical practice suggests to me that obsessionality frequently exists side by side with hysterical motifs in both men and women. Some women who are highly emotional may be obsessionals in sectors of their lives, especially around child-rearing and in the work place. And, while the intellectual realm was until recently primarily the domain of men, there have always been women with impressive intellects. But to openly support the validity of such differences today, as Harvard's ex-President Larry

---

39 Freud was jeered by his Viennese colleagues when he attempted to present a paper on a case of male hysteria, so anathema was the idea at the time.

Summers did when he suggested that men in general showed greater aptitude for math and science than women (which is true), is to risk losing your job, as Summers soon discovered.

The obsessional intellectual woman is a staple of modern society and in the psychotherapeutic consulting room. Some present to analysis with cool intellectualization, finding the analytical process "interesting," rather than emotionally transformative. They often report having been with their fathers and treated more like a "son than a daughter." Some purposefully seek out accomplished male analysts from whom they can "learn," in an effort at re-creating the earlier father-daughter intimacy. Many describe conflicted relationships with their mothers, who they are contemptuous of for having been "vague," "mixed-up," "incompetent," "cold," or "abandoning." The oedipal dynamic in the family is complex and psychologically incestuous.

Obsessional women, like obsessional men, are invested in their work. Some choose not to marry or to have children, whereas others attempt to fit children into an impossibly busy work schedule by juggling nannies and taking on excessive obligations at work and at home. Of the obsessional women who choose not to bear children, they may enjoy being close to children of others. They may be the "favorite aunt," or the best playmate of a friend's child. Their deep desire for attachment is, unfortunately, fraught with ambivalence and the fear of harming their own children by being an imperfect mother.

Others break down at the end of their childbearing years and choose to mother an artificially inseminated or adopted child.

A 38-year-old obsessional professional woman spent much of each therapy session talking about her marriage prospects. She was unable to identify a man that met her standards. The only men that appealed to her were either married or much older.

Her plan was to identify a sperm donor at age 40 and raise a child by herself, much to the dismay of her family.

WOMEN AND RELATIONSHIPS

Jung referred to *Eros* as the capacity for relationship, and suggested that, as a rule, women are more adept at it than men (C.G. Jung & Jaffe, 1959). Despite a reluctance to acknowledge biological differences as opposed to "constructed gender," there is good evidence that the capacity for attachment and relationship may be biologically hard-wired in women. Neurobiological observations suggest that maternal hypothalamic release of the hormone oxytocin plays a critical role in initiating attachment to the newborn infant (Sapolsky, 2017).

The willingness of women to prioritize relationship above other matters has been recognized through the ages. A joke describes Jesus chiding St. Peter for allowing sinners in through the gates of Heaven, to which Peter replies, "Lord, I send them away, but your mother lets them in through the back door!" Women traditionally have been more opposed to the imposition of strict boundaries than men, be they in relationships, the enforcement of laws, or setting national boundaries. In this regard, feminine priorities have infiltrated the Progressive movement, making it more likely to accept illegal behaviors than in the past. A recent example of this was the scandal surrounding the separation of young children from parents who had crossed the Southern border illegally. Despite repeated efforts by the Trump administration to explain that the separations were necessary and short-lived, and that the children were being treated well, and that the policy had been in place from before Trump's presidency, Progressive women were outraged, as they could imagine no higher priority than keeping mothers and children together. The fact that children are always separated from adult parents who have broken the law made no impact. Their outrage was quickly seconded by Progressive men, who pride themselves on being "woke" with respect to feminine demands.

Feminist author Carol Gilligan argued in *A Different Voice* that women are better at cooperating with others than men, making their decisions with greater consideration of how they affect the feelings of others (Gilligan, 1999). She criticized Kohlberg's standard argument that girls on average reach a lower level of moral development than boys (Kohlberg, 1981). She countered that, while boys may tend to favor a principled way of reasoning, moral arguments based on relationships are favored by girls.

Gillian's gender-based theory of morality maps well onto Sowell's constrained and unconstrained visions, and those between Christianity and Judaism with respect to law and social justice. According to Gilligan, there are two types of moral voice. The masculine voice is "logical and individualistic." It is primarily concerned with protecting the individual rights of people and ensuring that justice is done. By contrast, the female voice emphasizes the importance of compassionate care and the protecting of others. The overlap between the feminine vision and that of today's Progressivism is not a coincidence. The input of feminism has profoundly altered Progressive ideology.

WOMEN AND EMPATHY

Psychoanalysis has in recent years been less interested in Freud's one-body theory of mind that emphasizes intra-subjective dynamics, and has instead focused on the role of relational dynamics. This reflects a shift away from emphasis on the "father" to that of the "mother." Kohut's self-psychology emphasized the role of early empathic attunement between mother and infant in determining the adult's capacity to be empathic versus narcissistically absorbed, and infant psychological research has demonstrated the importance of empathic attunement and attachment between mothers and infants (Stern, 1985).

But what constitutes genuine empathy merits deeper consideration. Kohut referred to empathy as "vicarious introspection," meaning the psychological capacity to intuit accurately the experience of another (Kohut, 1971). This is not a simple task; it requires the ability to distinguish one's own feelings from that of another while at the same time discerning another's experience.

Empathy is not an equally shared innate capacity, and it cannot be learned in adulthood. Instead, it requires early education from an attuned mother and sufficient porosity between conscious and unconscious activities to discern the overtly expressed and implicit cues given off by others. As previously noted, intuition is weak in obsessionals and their ability to identify and name their own feeling states is also impaired. Consequently, their capacity for empathy is poor. Obsessional mothers project their own inner states inappropriately onto their children, producing repeated empathic failures. These early experiential failures may explain why obsessional women increasingly choose not to bear children for fear of repeating the cycle.

What the obsessional does exhibit is "sympathy" for others. Sympathy is based on projections of repressed memories of losses and abandonments. It is an asymmetric interpersonal dynamic that sees the child or others who are perceived as suffering as unduly vulnerable, the very experience that the obsessional consciously disavows for himself. By projecting it onto others, the obsessional can maintain distance and imaginal superiority from the sufferer.

Whereas such feelings are invariably part of the unconscious repertoire of obsessional women and men, they are reinforced by women's proclivity for relationship. But, when their own fear of abandonment is not consciously recognized, it inevitably distorts relationships with others. A psychoanalytic supervisor once counseled me that obsessional patients can resist therapeutic insight for years, but their fear of abandonment is so profound that once they enter therapy they rarely leave.

The following example elucidates how obsessional sympathy may be experienced by its recipient as condescension:

A young obsessional female physician was friendly with several "gay" men and chose to vacation overseas with one of them. She prided herself on being unprejudiced and supportive of her friend's gay life style. She found the behavior of gay men "amusing." But, when she returned from the trip, the man refused to have anything more to do with her. He claimed that her behavior on the trip was consistently condescending. She had no idea what he was referring to.

In this regard, many Conservative black voices have complained that they would like "sympathetic whites" to attend to their own issues and to leave theirs alone, as they experience the excessive good will of whites as condescension.

How does empathy differ from sympathy? The distinction has not been made systematically, but I will offer the following operative distinction. Genuine *empathy* includes the ability to intuit the mental experience of others accurately *and* to be genuinely concerned with *their* welfare. It is not empathic simply to intuit another's mental state. It is as or more important that the object of empathy *benefit* from being understood. Sympathy on the other hand often reflects mis-attunement, projection, and condescension. The sympathizer benefits primarily. Genuine empathy is therapeutic; sympathy is not.

Empathic concern is a cardinal feature of morality. It ideally considers both the individual and the welfare of the community. In a country based on law, as America has been traditionally, the rule of law must be dispassionate. It cannot favor the rich or yield in a biased fashion to the poor. The well-being of society must also be considered when empathy is properly applied. The recent debacle in the City of Seattle is a good example. The mayor's unwillingness to move the protesters out of their "Autonomous Zone" was not empathic. It was a condescending act of sympathy for the people of color leading the protest. There was no concern for the shop owners who were being terrorized in the inhabited area.

At times, punishment for bad behavior is empathic, as it recognizes the possibility that the individual may, at some level of dim awareness, *want* to behave properly, and that there is a need to discourage future bad behaviors. There is a place in society for tough love when it is based in genuine concern. Unfortunately, this notion has been abandoned by many to the detriment of child-rearing and society.

Newspapers regularly report on serious crimes committed in America that either go unpunished or lightly so. Progressives are inclined to coddle lawbreakers, aliens, and minorities because they perceive them as disadvantaged. This is neither "justice" nor empathy; instead, it is immoral. In a recent case in liberal Boston, a young African man, here on temporary visa, was convicted of engaging in two bank robberies in which he threatened to kill people in the bank if he did not get the money he was seeking. He was apprehended, allowed to plea bargain, and served a brief sentence for a serious crime so that he would not have to face mandatory deportation as a felon. Shortly after being released back into society, he brutally murdered two young Boston physicians in their apartment. Unfortunately, crimes like this occur with some regularity in Progressive America but are rarely advertised by the Progressive media, as they undermine the Progressive narrative that illegal aliens are peaceful contributors to American society. The victims are rarely considered in the calculus of Progressives because of their desire to forgive others out of a misguided sense of neurotic guilt.

The ill-conceived sympathy for people of color and the poor by what is often a well-to-do obsessional elite is, in fact, a guise for the latter's guised contempt for these groups. Until this is realized, Progressive Americans will continue to ignore their own "reaction formations" and project their guised contempt onto others. That means that innocent Americans will continue to be victimized by Progressives' neurotic predilections.

The argument that most illegal aliens are law-abiding does not merit serious consideration. The law is capable of distinguishing those who seriously break the law from those who are law-abiding. There should be zero tolerance for those who have committed serious crimes, regardless of their race or immigrant status. The fact that illegal aliens are here illegally should not be ignored as though the law is meaning-less. If the "feminine" psyche is unable to make "principled" rather than "relational" decisions, then perhaps it might be best for "relational" types, be they men or women, to avoid working in the legal system or as lawmakers until they are willing to bear the responsibility for the fate of innocents who are victimized as the result of their misguided leniency. In addition, the Progressive press that repeatedly hides crimes from public view because they challenge Progressive ideology must bear responsibility for failing to report facts so the public can make its own conclusions concerning the state of America's judicial system. The First Amendment that extends freedom to the press was not designed for a press that suppresses the truth from the public.

As previously noted, Orthodox Judaism and some conservative Christian denominations have different approaches to social justice than those that espouse Progressive ideology that poorly reflects the actual tenets of their religion. It is worthwhile considering the ideas of Rabbi Joseph Soloveitchik, one of the major thinkers in Judaism in the 20th CE on this issue. In his musings on the subject of justice, Soloveitchik scrutinizes the difference between secular morality and religious morality from the perspective of traditional Judaism.

As he argues (Soloveichik, 2005) :

There is a law against theft.... Everyone assents to such a law... every normal person is repelled by the ugliness of the act.... No one will approve of stealing candy from a baby or money from a beggar. But what about another sort of theft, which was depicted so often in literature, particularly by Victor Hugo in *Les Miserables*? A poor man, just out of prison, with no prospects, steals a loaf of bread from a bakery in order to sustain his life. The proprietor of the bakery...will not suffer. The loss incurred is infinitesimal. Why punish the poor starving man? Is it a crime or is it not a crime?... If my conscience is the final arbiter...I would set him free.... But stealing was forbidden by the Almighty...whether we understand it or not.... Rabbi Akiva maintained that man must not rely solely on his morals and sensitivities, even pertaining to civil law.... This is the basic reason why secular ethics has failed (Soloveitchik, *Pesach*, p. 245).

From this perspective, Gilligan's notion of feminine relational morality is at best a partial one that fails to achieve the fullness of a principled morality.

WHERE HAVE THE MEN GONE?

Prior to the emergence of the feminist movement, child care was generally divided asymmetrically between parents. Studies show that this continues to be the case, although men have taken a greater role in the day-to-day activities of child care. In the traditional family, mothers stayed at home raising children, while fathers went to work to provide for their family.

The splitting of roles allowed for the presentation of two distinct voices, although it also created conflicts about child-rearing when parents could not agree on how best to raise a child. This parental configuration is no longer prevalent. The divorce rate has risen dramatically in the last 50 years, although it recently has begun to stabilize. Many children are currently raised in one-parent families, usually by mothers, with infrequent or no opportunity for fathering. This is particularly true in the African-American community, where single family households account for 75% of all families (C. Murray, 1999). According to the CDC data from 2011-2013, a high percentage of women aged 25-34 (81.6%) agreed with the statement, "It is okay for an unmarried female to have and raise a child" (Statistics, 2014).

Many young men have been co-opted by the aims of feminism and the Progressive movement. They have been convinced that to challenge the Progressive feminine agenda is *prima facie* evidence of misogyny, another variant of "racism." As Gilligan notes, if only the traditional male voice is expressed, then softer elements of masculinity are lost. But to hear only the feminine voice means that the tougher elements of masculinity are lost as well; certainly, this does not result in a "diversity" of opinions. Instead, it produces a monolithic perspective, in which the male voice is discouraged and finally no longer heard.

Child-rearing has become increasingly "emasculated." Even when two-parent families remain intact, there has been a shift in perspective that views both parents as contributing "equally" to the nurturing of children, but with both assuming the feminine voice and its uncon-strained vision. Difficulties in setting limits is likely the greatest cause of the increase in narcissistic entitlement that we have witnessed over the last 40 years for America's youth.

Traditionally, it was a primary role of fathers to encourage the separation of male children from their mothers. In the past, this was mediated by prescribed rites of passage, but these no longer exist in America. This leaves young men with few examples of what the mas-culine voice sounds like, and few outlets for expressing a version of masculinity that is distinct from feminine conceptions of what it *should* look like.

Obsessional parenting has both parents preoccupied with providing a "safe" and "supportive" environment for their children. Unlike in the past, new parents have become highly attuned to the potential negative consequences of psychological trauma in childhood. Obsessional par-ents attempt to protect their children *perfectly*. This so-called "helicop-ter parenting" is an amusing term for a seriously pathological parenting style.[40] These parents may be termed *narci-pathogenic*. Mothers, and in many cases, both parents, coddle their children, intrude in their activi-ties at home and outside the house, "help" them do *their* homework, and participate in virtually all of their decision-making. The child senses the underlying anxieties of obsessional parents and incorporates them via "osmosis." As Jung said:

The little world of childhood with its familiar surroundings is
a model of the greater world. The more intensively the family

---

40 Certainly, obsessional parenting is not limited to America. I recently returned from a trip to Finland, where I heard a about "curling" parents. Curling is a sport in which a large stone is slid down the ice with a team of "sweepers" who, with brooms, frantically try to guide the stone to its goal. Different term; same phenomenon.

has stamped its character upon the child, the more it will tend to feel and see its earlier miniature world again in the bigger world of adult life. Naturally this is not a conscious, intellectual process (C.G. Jung, 1962).

Motivated by their obsessional parents' need to control, and by fears of making mistakes rather than becoming independent, children become anxious and insecure. They fail to develop a "true self," as Winnicott termed it, and ultimately either assume the narcissistic and obsessional styles of their parents or rebel against them (D. Winnicott, 1960). In the absence of realistic feedback, appropriate criticism, exposure to reasonable dangers, or the opportunity to experience failure, a child cannot be expected to mature into a healthy, responsible adult.

Winnicott recognized that there is no such thing as "a baby," and that it is the dynamic between the infant and the caretaker that matters with respect to child development. But, when the normal female narcissism that fosters early attachment to the infant extends beyond the time when separation is optimally required, the result is a narcissistically disturbed child.

Furthermore, this failure to separate is particularly harmful for male children who need to identify with the male role. But some feminists argue vigorously against roles. They encourage women to be more like men, and men more like women. The result of this approach is not the ideal androgyne. Instead, it tends to produce women who are overwhelmed by attempting to bear too much responsibility, and men who are psychologically emasculated and cannot succeed in a non-maternal world.

We are currently seeing the end results of disastrous parenting. Hopelessly immature and fearful college students are demanding "safe" zones. At an age when they should be learning to confront challenges on their own, they instead insist on being protected from all manner of adversity by university administrators. Inordinately sensitive to criticism, these young people exhibit the obsessional features of immaturity, emotional avoidance, and inability to make decisions. The situation is aggravated by continued interference of doting parents who may threaten to withhold donations to private universities unless their children's demands are met and the capitulation of Progressive teachers afraid to confront the ill-conceived demands of students and parents who agree with them. The academic world has been largely co-opted by the Progressive agenda and administrators who stand by, idly permitting the disruptive behaviors of entitled students, thereby encouraging even worse behaviors in the future. Progressive educators are unwilling to enforce boundaries or to force students to deal with adversity in a mature way. As they are also devoted to eradicating meritocracy, including an evaluating grading system, many students believe they have found a comfortable new home in Progressive ideology.

When today I see young men and women in their teens and twenties protesting on the streets of America, angry and ill-educated, tearing down statues of its leaders yet unable to clearly express the reason for their hostility, I don't see a mob of committed Marxists; instead, I see a dismal failure of America's Progressive parents to raise autonomous adults and good citizens.

MAN-BASHING

Freud referred to "penis envy" as the desire of women to assume what they perceived as the more powerful masculine role in society. The concept has been enormously unpopular among many feminists. But it is hard to dismiss in the face of the hostile and unjust accusations that have been leveled at men in recent years by women. The concerns of some ardent Progressive feminists concerning the influence of men on society have led to unfounded accusations of sexual misconduct and misogyny by male teachers and students on college campuses. Political correctness has made it virtually impossible to criticize women without being confronted with accusations of misogyny. In response, young men have learned to acquiesce to the desires of women and, in too many cases, have adopted mannerisms that are excessively soft:

> A 47-year-old liberal Progressive obsessional man had difficulties maintaining relationships with women. He was careful to be an empathic listener and tried hard to meet their desires in relationship. Despite his kindness, these women invariably left him, complaining that he was "too soft." Some of them treated him frankly sadistically.

Obsessional and overly compliant men think that it is politically correct for them to provide vocal support to feminist causes. Unfortunately, too often this includes impeaching their own masculinity and accepting guilt imposed by feminist ideologues for being a "man." These men perceive their proper role to be "sensitive." Certainly, integrating these qualities into traditional masculine psychology has its advantages, but it is misguided if it results in the abrogation of positive masculine attributes.

SEX VERSUS GENDER

The question of what determines gender, nature versus nurture, is complex and currently cannot be answered accurately, but neither is it a total mystery. The idea that feminine behavior is in large measure biologically determined and beyond one's control has been vehemently rejected by some ardent Progressive feminists, despite scientific evidence to the contrary. They reject the limits imposed by biology, arguing with some degree of paranoia that "sex" is a concept adopted by men specifically to limit the potential of women. Their concerns extend to transsexuals who wish to adopt the contra-sexual role. As a rule, feminists tend to support gender-based issues, including homosexuality, same-sex marriage, and the use of public bathrooms by transsexuals in America. In October of 2015, the Chicago Tribune ran the following news item:

> The battle for equal access for transgender students is pitting Illinois' largest high school district against federal authorities. At issue is locker room access for a transgender high school student in Palatine-based Township High School District 211. The student, who identifies as female, is asking that she receive full access to the girls' locker room. Citing privacy concerns, the district has denied the request and instead offered a separate room where the student can change. "At some point, we have to balance the privacy rights of 12,000 students with other particular, individual needs of another group of students," said District 211 Superintendent Daniel Cates. "We believe this infringes on the privacy of all the students that we serve."
>
> But an official with the American Civil Liberties Union, which is representing the student in a complaint filed with the U.S. Department of Education, called the district's stance "blatant discrimination, no matter how the district tries to couch it." Federal officials responded to the complaint, which was filed about a year and a half ago with the Department of Education's Office for Civil Rights, by saying the school is in violation of the Title IX gender equality law, according to the ACLU and district officials.

The proposition that the rights of transsexuals — a minute percentage of Americans who, until recently, were rarely seen in public — takes precedence over the reasonable concerns of the clear majority of heterosexuals, is mind-boggling for many. But the definition of sex, which until recently had been objectively based on genitalia and secondary sexual characteristics, has been systematically ignored by Progressives, and a new definition based solely on individual subjectivity has replaced it.

This is disturbing at several levels. The fact is that most, if not all, transsexuals are suffering psychologically from a fixed delusion, which is the accepted psychiatric definition of a limited psychosis. The Progressive left chooses to ignore this. One might conclude that those who offer the Progressive argument that reality is imaginally constructed, and with it little to no basis in the physical realm, have become unhinged from reality.

This topic extends to a host of so-called "gender preferences," so that, in theory on any given day, individuals can decide for themselves whether they are heterosexual or homosexual, men or women, or anything in between. Psychiatrists have long recognized that individuals are located on a spectrum between heterosexuality and homosexuality without needing to name the entire spectrum of possibilities. The liberal Progressive city of New York currently *officially* recognizes 31 different terms for gender. Based on the absurdity of this lengthy list, how is a sane person to take the Progressive agenda concerning gender seriously? Yet it has become a serious issue, with penalties for those who reject it.

The fact that the Obama Justice Department presumed to institute punitive measures against those who opposed the sharing of bathrooms was, to traditional-minded individuals, both a travesty of justice and evidence of undue interference by the federal government into the private domain. Heterosexuals who objected to using bathrooms that anyone can use with impunity were recently told by Maura Healey, the lesbian attorney general of Massachusetts that, if they didn't like it, they could "hold it." On his first day in office, President Trump cancelled the Obama Executive order and gave the choice with respect to bathroom rights back to the individual states to determine.

But what is disturbing to many Americans is that, instead of confronting the serious problems the country is facing, Progressives are immersed in a host of issues that are of marginal importance. This reflects their narrow obsessional focus.

IDENTITY POLITICS

The convergence of feminism with racial politics has created a "perfect storm" for Progressive ideology. Historically, the great sin of America was the institution of slavery. Slavery was an established institution at the time of the founding of America, particularly in the Southern colonies, where cheap labor was required for large plantations. The Founding Fathers were aware of the problem, and a compromise was reached at the Constitutional Congress that allowed slavery to persist in the southern states but valued slaves as 3/5 of a man with respect to representation in Congress. It is often misstated that this was the result of the prejudice of the Founders when, in fact, it was the Northern states' way of limiting the power of the Southern states to legislate the spread of slavery into new territories.

The Civil War was fought in large measure to determine the fate of slavery in America. In 1862, Abraham Lincoln freed the slaves with the Emancipation Proclamation. But legally supported racial prejudice and separation of the races in public sites continued in some American states into the mid-20th CE, when it was outlawed by aggressive civil rights legislation, backed by executive action, enforced by the National Guard in some instances.

Today, few can legitimately argue that great progress has not been made on racial issues in America. As David Horowitz notes, "Far from being racists, Americans are the most tolerant people on the planet" and he quotes William H. Frey's statistics from the Brookings Institute to support his conclusion:

Sociologists have traditionally viewed multiracial marriages as a benchmark of the ultimate assimilation of a particular group into society. Black-white marriages were still illegal in 16 states in 1967. A 1968 Gallup poll found that only 4% of Americans approved of black-white marriages. Today that number is 87%. In 1960, of all marriages by blacks, only 1.7% were black-white. Today, it's 12% and rising (Horowitz, *Big*, p. 25).

When this is considered together with the increased representation of African-Americans in all walks of American life, it's hard to justify why the Progressive left insists that white America is racist. There is little evidence to support that viewpoint.

Women, until recently, rightfully viewed themselves as disadvantaged with respect to men. Consequently, it was not a great leap for the feminist movement to identify and support the struggles of racial minorities to eradicate prejudice. The convergence of feminism with the civil rights movement has been the primary mover of today's Progressive social justice agenda. Both groups want to wrest power from American white men by whatever means necessary. They have vocally argued that white men who do not accede to their demands are "racists," even if they have never behaved in a racially prejudicial manner.

As it is simply not possible to be entirely devoid of unconscious evaluations of difference, such accusations are unjust. *No one* can honestly state that he or she is totally devoid of bias, and Progressives appear to have little problem denigrating white men and Conservatives of both sexes. It is also possible to hold certain biases and still behave fairly and without prejudice toward others. Few women or blacks who are qualified find themselves rejected for employment, loans, or other transactions in today's America. Indeed, in many Progressive settings, they may be at a distinct advantage with respect to gaining admissions to universities and employment. But qualifications *do* matter, especially for those who are in the business of lending money. If you are unemployed with a terrible credit score, you can expect, like anyone else, to be turned away by a lending institution. If you have no college degree and limited skills, you can expect to encounter difficulties finding a well-paying good job whether you are black or white, man or woman.

Furthermore, bias cuts both ways. Affirmative action rules that favor certain minorities to the exclusion of others are fundamentally biased. Whereas affirmative action may have played an important role back in the 1960s to jump-start a system that had long been biased, there is no place for it in a society where institutional prejudice is no longer determinative, either in the academy or the workplace. Affirmative action policies currently serve to promote racial difference and are biased against non-black minorities. Certain minority groups, including Asian-Americans, have found themselves penalized for their hard work by seeing merit-based positions awarded to less qualified peoples of color. These biases contribute to the hostilities that surround identity politics. In the past, America prospered as a meritocracy and it should return to that tradition as soon as possible so that genuine integration into American society can occur.

Progressives err, be they white or black, men or women, in suggesting that *they* are not racists. Progressives openly preach bigotry and racism against white men with impunity on university campuses. Efforts to engage them in constructive conversation invariably result in recriminations against white men. Rather than admit that America has made substantial progress in the arena of civil rights, Progressives choose to portray America as a racist country. As Horowitz says (Horowitz, 2017):

> The real effect of calling people racists is to drum them out of the company of decent people and to stigmatize them as "extremists, social outcasts and unsuitable to participate in any legitimate conversation. It is because America is not a racist society that racists — at least white racists — are hateful (Horowitz, *Big*, p. 5).

This reflects the psychology of envy and victimization. By remaining perpetually aggrieved, victims resist accepting responsibility for their own failures and instead exhibit prejudice against those they envy. The fact is that the sympathetic and covert condescending stance of Progressives toward blacks has been disastrous. In large cities, 60 years after the Civil Rights Act, many African-Americans continue to reside in ghettoes ridden with poverty and high levels of violent crime, most of it perpetrated by blacks against other blacks. Few homes have two parents and the unemployment rate is near 50% (C. Murray, 1999).

African-Americans who, based on demographic statistics, had begun to make economic progress in the early 20th CE when they still lived predominantly in intact families have, since the institution of the federal Progressive civil rights policies in the 1960s, become largely dependent on government welfare support. The result has been the development of an urban racial underclass that no longer participates actively in the workforce, lives with little hope and, more importantly, has few economic opportunities due to an educational system that refuses to realistically assess individuals and train them for appropriate employment (C. Murray, 2008).

There have always been children left behind, as there are real and frankly insurmountable differences in the intellectual capacities of different people. Progressive politicians lacking genuine concern have abused urban blacks for years to suit their own political ends, yet many African-Americans are disinclined to recognize the harm that has been done to them, as it would also require them to assume responsibility for their own future and, as importantly, to shed their grievances against white America for historical injustices that occurred in the past and therefore cannot be undone. Real progress and mental health require that aggrieved people mourn their losses and move on, as Freud concludes in *Mourning and Melancholia* (S. Freud, 1959).[41]

Furthermore, some black Progressive politicians promote anger against whites for financial gain. Perennial opportunists, such as the Reverend Al Sharpton and Jesse Jackson, can be counted on to stir up anti-white and anti-American sentiment among African-Americans in any situation in which blacks are harmed, even when they are at fault.

One of the extraordinary features of the last presidential campaigns was candidate Donald Trump's promise to raise the standards of urban blacks by providing them with increased economic opportunity. Trump questioned the effects of Democratic leadership on the black community, and asked the seminal question of "What do you have to lose" by ridding yourselves of liberal Progressive policies that have produced no tangible benefit in America's ghettoes for 60 years? The response

---

41 Religions have recognized this fact and there are days of mourning that commemorate losses each year, helping to ritualize the process. The Jewish fast day of Tisha B'Av commemorates the destruction of the two Jerusalem Temples but has also, over time, integrated other great losses. Perhaps a Martin Luther King Day should be observed not merely as a holiday and commemoration of his assassination but a day in which Americans mourn the losses of African-Americans over the time that they were enslaved and denigrated in America. This might alleviate some of the resentment that lingers in the black community and inhibits their progress.

by both white and black Progressives was to attack Trump viciously for being a "racist," the label routing applied to anyone who dares to question the Progressive agenda. Trump delivered on his promise and, prior to the coronavirus' devastating economic effects, unemployment for blacks, Hispanics, and women had reached historical lows.

Despite what appeared to be clear progress in racial relations over the last 60 years, Barack Obama was party to a serious deterioration in American race relations. Far left-leaning and quasi-terrorist groups such as "Black Lives Matters" have foisted a false narrative of persistent prejudice and violence against blacks that targets white police. However, as journalist Heather Mac Donald documents in the *War on Cops,* evidence to support their claims is impossible to substantiate (Mac Donald, 2016). Much of it, like the false narrative that fostered the Ferguson riots in 2015, is pure fabrication. But Obama and Progressive leaders, rather than accepting factual errors in the narratives of the radical left and calling for an end to violence against police, chose instead to support the demonstrators and to invite the leaders of *Black Lives Matter* to the White House as honored guests, thereby affirming their support for more potential violence against law enforcement.

No one can claim that there are not bigoted and racist people in America; that will always be the case. What is critical is that Progressives stop accusing America at large of being so, because that is simply a lie and no honest politician or journalist should continue giving credence to it. But that is what Barack Obama, Hillary Clinton, Democratic leaders, and the Progressive press continue to do, and they experienced an angry backlash in the 2016 election from those Americans who knew that. Unfortunately, this false and harmful propaganda will only disappear when people begin to behave responsibly.

Most of the violent crimes directed against blacks are perpetrated by other blacks in urban areas. The city of Chicago has witnessed thousands of murders over the last 10 years, with virtually no concern expressed by *Black Lives Matter,* the mainstream media, ex-President Obama, or Progressive politicians, most notably the ex-mayor of Chicago, Rahm Emmanuel. Obsessional Progressives have managed to convince themselves of the veracity of these claims, even when faced with mounds of data that repudiate them. Avoiding the truth allows them to cling to their false obsessional ideology of moral superiority in the face of rampant prejudice.

Charles Murray poignantly traces the history of identity politics in *Losing Ground* (C. Murray, 1984).

> Race is central to the problem of reforming social policy, not because it is intrinsically so but because the debate about what to do has been perverted by the underlying consciousness among whites that "they" — the people to be helped by social policy — are predominantly black, and blacks are owed a debt. The result was that the intelligentsia and the policymakers, coincident with the revolution in social policy, began treating the black poor in ways that they would never consider treating people they respected. Is the black crime rate skyrocketing? Look at the black criminal's many grievances against society. Are black illegitimate birth rates five times those of whites? We must remember that blacks have a much broader view of the family than we do and aunts and grandmothers fill in. Did black labor force participation among the young plummet? We can hardly blame someone for having too much pride to work at a job sweeping floors. Are black high-school graduates illiterate? The educational system is insensitive. Are their test scores a hundred points lower than others? The tests are biased. Do black youngsters lose jobs to white youngsters because their

mannerisms and language make them incomprehensible to their prospective employers? The culture of the ghetto has its own validity (Murray, *Losing* , p. 222).

Murray recognizes that this behavior is nothing less than concealed contempt supported by the crudest form of psychological denial.

Chapter 8: Mis-Education

The purpose of education is to replace an empty mind with an open one.

— Malcolm Forbes

Many young people today are frightened and angry with anyone who challenges their worldview. As journalist Gregg Lukianoff and psychologist Jonathan Heidt remark in their article, *The Coddling of the American Mind* (Lukianoff & Haidt, 2016):

> Something strange is happening at America's colleges and universities. A movement is arising, undirected and driven largely by students, to scrub campuses clean of words, ideas, and subjects that might cause discomfort or give offense. Last December, Jeannie Suk wrote an online article for the New Yorker about law students asking her professors at Harvard not to teach rape law — or, in one case, even use the word "violate" (as in "that violates the law") lest it cause students distress (Lukianoff and Heidt, *Coddling*, p. 1).

Hopefully, this sounds ludicrous, but it is a genuine problem for those who do not agree with Progressive pedagogy. Consider the experience of a patient of mine who is a scholar at a local university:

> I can no longer teach what I want. There is little regard for my area of scholarship. The new female chair of my department insists that our curriculum must include only subjects that are societally "relevant." Seniority and accomplishment count for nothing. I am afraid to speak up at staff meetings, lest I be criticized or lose my job.

This is the current state of higher education. As Murray notes, many universities currently offer courses limited to several hours a day, Tuesday through Thursday, with Mondays and Fridays as free days. There are no week-end classes. There are few introductory survey courses to broad areas of scholarship. Students are free to pick their curriculum and frequently simply search for the least demanding courses required to graduate (C. Murray, 2008). There are virtually no conservative voices to be heard on many large university campuses, and protests regularly break out, as they did when conservatives like Murray, author Ann Coulter, or Secretary of Education Betsy DeVos were invited to speak on college campuses. A Progressive teacher who was physically hurt by marauding students and subsequently hospitalized during a protest against Murray, when asked who she thought was responsible for her injuries, responded "Donald Trump!" This behavior, both uncivil and aggressive, undermines the exercise of free speech in America, which had traditionally been one of the greatest virtues of American higher education.

Young people seek out "safe zones" where they can be protected from speech they perceive as "aggressive." One is reminded of the ancient tale of how young Prince Siddhartha, the Buddha, was sheltered by his father from the realities of pain, disease and death, and had to abandon his secure environment to seek out his own undisguised experience of the world.[42]

Murray points out that the curriculum of American public schools is currently largely devoid of any substantive content and brings examples of the curricula from both public and private schools. The public school curriculum is primarily dedicated to Progressive social justice issues and hardly touches on the factual content required to produce an educated citizen (C. Murray, 2008). A disturbing number of public high school graduates cannot name the vice-president of the United States, do not know what the Supreme Court does, cannot name the capital of Texas, or find China on a map. More perplexing is the fact that few appear to be embarrassed by their lack of knowledge or appear to care at all. It is not possible to maintain a democracy comprised of illiterate citizens.

A young mother with a young boy in grade school complained to me in therapy that her son came home from school and proclaimed that President Obama was a "great" president because he supported the LGBT community. The mother, who holds conservative values in a predominantly Progressive community, asked where he learned that and was told the teacher had spent the last week discussing how President Obama was protecting everybody's rights in the country. The mother does not share this sentiment, and wants her child to be learning facts, not opinions, and is at a loss as to how to educate her son.

The seemingly benign aims of televised programs for children in the 1970s, including "Sesame Street," "Mr. Rogers," the popular messages of the MTV generation, the widespread availability of escapist video games, and social media pressures, together with an unchallenged Progressive agenda in public and many private schools, have converged to produce a generation of young adults with uniformly

---

42 Interestingly, it was only through Siddharta's confrontation with the real world that he became the compassionate Buddha.

hypersensitive attitudes about political correctness and distorted perceptions of social injustice. Furthermore, as they are rarely provided with real facts, and have not been exposed to the art of debate, they cannot support their opinions and must regress to name calling as a defense when challenged.

"Millennials" who are now coming of age are genuinely afraid of what will happen to them under the new Trump administration, which does not seem inclined to coddle them. Their hysteria has been enacted on American streets, university campuses, and on the sets of Hollywood "glitter" events.[43] These expressions of hysteria are unquestionably real, but it is difficult for those who express their abhorrence of the Trump administration to explain rationally what the objective basis of their fear is. Instead, attempts at dialogue rapidly degenerate into derisive labeling of those who oppose them. These young people apparently expect the new Trump administration to jail all immigrants and Muslims, attack college students, return blacks to the plantation, destroy the earth by ignoring global warming, and then impulsively push the nuclear button and destroy the planet.

But at least half of the country does not share these concerns. People, including media journalists, seen crying hysterically after Trump's election, appear to be suffering from delusional ideation. That is not surprising as they have essentially been brainwashed at school and by a relentless Progressive-biased press. They have grown to believe that all of what they fear is likely to transpire as long as Trump is president. The mental health community has also been coopted by Progressivism and political correctness. It has banded together online and in publications to question the mental health of the president, which violates the

---

43 At a recent event following President Trump's election, "Madonna" talked about her desire to "blow up the White House." Had that remark been made concerning President Obama or by a non-celebrity, the chances are they might have been interviewed by either the Secret Service or FBI, as well they should be. Remarks like this should not go unpunished or at least investigated. Free speech does not extend to making threats against a sitting president.

"Goldwater rule" of the American Psychiatric Association that states that it is unethical for psychiatrists to make diagnostic claims without having personally interviewed a person and without their consent.[44] In many cases, they have taken to social media to complain about the genuine fears of their patients encumbered by Trump's election, while appearing to be oblivious and unconcerned for those patients who find the current politically correct climate in America very disturbing. The claim that President Donald Trump is narcissistic is unquestionably true, but that diagnosis is so widely applicable to politicians in Washington, D.C. that one would have to recall all of Congress if that were to be the criteria for removing a politician from office.

In this age of the "therapeutic," young people are being raised to be unnecessarily fearful. This is contributing to their anxious obsessionality. There may be nothing more important for the future of America than to address what young students are being taught in our schools. Virtually all religious traditions have recognized that early education is critical in shaping the ideas of the young. Fundamentalist religionists would not dream of allowing their children to be "tainted" by the ideas of modern secular society in a modern public school. In most cases, their approach of parochial or home schooling has the desired result. As the Jesuit, St. Xavier, reportedly claimed, *"Give me the children until they are seven, and anyone may have them afterward."*

John Dewey, one of the early proponents of Progressive public education, recognized that the aims of Progressivism would have to be transmitted to the young via government-controlled public education (Nugent, 2010). This represents one of the major objections that

---

44 I am old enough to remember the Democratic commercials showing a mushroom cloud and the question of whether Barry Goldwater, the Conservative senator from Arizona, was mentally stable and should be allowed the nuclear access codes. Goldwater lost in a landslide to Johnson, but Congress subsequently adopted a law that it was unethical for mental health professionals to diagnosis politicians of standing with a mental disease without having assessed them in person and without their consent.

Progressives have toward charter schools and religious education in this country. The success of Progressivism requires that children be indoctrinated from a young age into its ideology and that the central government retain control of the process.

Progressive education is mandated by the federal government to meet educational goals that reduce emphasis on intellectual differences between children. Whereas in earlier times, talented children were promoted to their level of capacity, this rarely occurs today in public schools. Instead, public education is oriented more toward "ethical improvement" than achieving academic scholarship. School curricula are configured to serve the needs of minorities and those judged as intellectually disadvantaged. Whereas caring for the disadvantaged is an important aspect of the public educational process in a compassionate society, denying genuine differences should not be.

The curriculum in universities promotes minority studies while devaluing the time-honored classical canon that has been the source of the greatness of Western civilization; it has been rejected as prejudiced toward the "white establishment" (D'Souza, 1991). College courses focus on black and Hispanic studies, gay and transsexual rights, etc. Achieving racial diversity has become the primary goal of many Progressive academic and other liberal businesses and institutions, whether it can be evidentially demonstrated to improve the performance of these institutions or not. One might sympathize with such a stance in a school system of another country, but why, other than for masochistic reasons, would Americans choose to undermine their own proven success? Why would American President Barack Obama want to start his tenure in office with an "apology tour" to the Middle East, especially following the events of 9/11? Consider his remarks on April 6, 2009 to the Turkish Parliament:

The United States is still working through some of our darker periods in history. Facing the Washington Monument that I spoke of is a memorial of Abraham Lincoln, the man who freed those who were enslaved even after Washington led our Revolution. Our country still struggles with the legacies of slavery and segregation, the past treatment of Native Americans.

All interesting and perhaps true, but was the president ignorant of the continuing human rights abuses occurring in Turkey and other parts of the Arab world? In a country where conquest was final and slavery common, why would he imagine that there would be a sympathetic reaction from a non-democratic nation with fundamentalist Islamic leanings? Only an obsessional ideologue like Obama could be so seriously out of touch with reality.

Students are being encouraged to adopt values that neither conform to facts nor serve the future interests of American society. The idea of American exceptionalism with primacy on the world stage is systematically undermined by the Progressive agenda, which appears to be more interested in reducing America's political and economic influence in the world while paradoxically serving the economic interests of a globalist elite.[45] Students are taught to believe that America is racist, bellicose, and immoral, rather than the beacon of freedom that it has been for much of the world. America's young are indoctrinated into a mindset that encourages them to accept guilt for the past wrongdoings of others, who lived in different times and other social contexts.

Indeed, one of the most extraordinary transgressions of the current Progressive movement is its willingness to reject historical figures for

---

45 Mr. Obama recently accepted a $500K fee for a single speech. Despite his stated concerns about global warming and rising sea levels, he has purchased a multi-million dollar house on the beach of Martha's Vineyard. This is his right, but how does it jibe with his Progressive concerns about income inequality and the poor? It is doubtful that he will be providing an honest answer to that question anytime soon.

moral infractions that were widely practiced in their time. Founders like Washington and Jefferson are denounced as "slave holders;" students insist that Woodrow Wilson's name be removed from the Princeton School of Politics for his racist views. Any historian of merit would condemn such anachronistic applications of current values to individuals who lived in earlier and different times. But liberal Progressive "scholars" appear to not understand this basic fact of the science of historical studies.[46] Today, there is a concerted effort to erase all of American history and to replace it with a fanciful story about how America was built by minorities, or at least on their backs. Columbus is vilified for having discovered America and disturbed the imagined idyllic lives of indigenous Native Americans. Unfortunately, there is not a shred of truth to any of this.

Obsessional emphasis on minority rights, on the bathroom rights of transsexuals, promoting diversity in the armed forces, on the American diet, on certain environmental concerns, all suggest an exceedingly narrow vision for America. Parents who send their children to public or secular day schools may not be fully aware of what the Progressive educational agenda is at these institutions. Questions of diversity, sexual preference, sexual education, are all standard fare. In some public schools within the inner cities, the ability to read at what had formally been considered a level of competence has been severely compromised. More than half of 8th grade students cannot answer basic simple tests of reading comprehension or reason mathematically. All of what had traditionally been considered required learning has become optional or designed to satisfy the lowest acceptable standard (C. Murray, 2008).

---

46 I recognize that certain symbols may be disturbing to minorities in this country. However, they are part of the evolving history of this country. The systematic removal of Southern heroes of the Civil War is no different than the systematic erasures of previous leaders in totalitarian nations. The expunging of memory is part of revisionist history. The death camp at Auschwitz-Birkenau still stands as a reminder of real history and a real Holocaust. How much easier it might be to tear it down.

Are students being brainwashed into Progressive ideology within America's public schools? The answer is undoubtedly *yes,* and the primary method being used is political correctness, an idea that developed in Maoist Communist China (Hughes, 2010). None of this bodes well for America's future. Rather than being challenged to think independently, young students are being inculcated into "groupthink." To be fair, education is virtually always a form of brainwashing as young minds are easily influenced, and no American should be educated to ignore the misdeeds of its country, as genuine patriotism is not blind. But, in the case of America, its misdeeds are balanced, if not greatly exceeded, by its virtues. This is what should be taught if education is meant to train fine minds, not ideologies. But, more importantly, an objective introduction to American history and governmental procedures based primarily on facts and not on the roles of people of color or women would do much to improve the attitudes and knowledge of young America citizens. There is far more to American history than slavery and misogyny. A young mother in analysis bemoaned the educational choices available to her adolescent son about to attend high school:

I'm not a liberal. My husband and I share conservative values. We are finding it impossible to identify a private high school that is not immersed in the "politically correct" agenda. Forget the public schools; they are totally out of consideration. I've toured several private high schools and can't find one whose bulletin boards are not plastered with politically correct slogans. I frankly don't know what to do. We didn't want to send him to parochial or military school but these may be the only options left to us. The public schools are out of the question.

They have embraced the politically correct agenda lock, stock, and barrel!

Curiously, despite the ubiquitous tentacles of political correctness, young ideologues comfortably behind closed doors manage to watch movies and YouTube videos and listen to music that includes the most vulgar types of misogyny, bigotry, racism, and violence. Something is wrong with this picture. It appears to be a fear of being criticized in public. These paradoxical behaviors speak to the obsessional psychology that belies political correctness.

CHAPTER 9: THE OBSESSIONAL ELITE AND THE CULTURE WARS

The best argument against democracy is a five-minute conversation with the average voter.

— Winston Churchill.

Incestuous, homogenous fiefdoms of self-proclaimed expertise are always rank-closing and mutually self-defending, above all else.

— Glenn Greenwald

Some years ago, I began to encounter a new type of medical student. They were intelligent and serious, but hypersensitive to criticism.[47] Although they came from diverse ethnic backgrounds, they shared a high degree of homogeneity with respect to their previous education and life experiences. Most had attended private preparatory schools and Ivy League universities, and were now enrolled at a world-class medical school. Many had taken a 'gap year' after graduating college to do charitable work in Africa, or on an Indian reservation, or they had participated in an altruistic social assistance or education program. Their credentials on paper were stellar. As medical schools are currently essentially closed to anyone without a near-perfect academic record, a long list of extracurricular accomplishments is required for admission, so such resumes were not unusual.

47 Saul Alinsky commented that it was critical that political organizers maintain a good sense of humor, another point that eludes the obsessional left.

Elite medical schools encourage "over-achieving." Some first-year medical students had already created start-up businesses or made important medical research findings while working over the summers in research laboratories. Yet, in other respects, most of these talented young people were profoundly immature and insulated. They rarely associated in any meaningful way with those outside their own elite class. Even when they ventured out into the "third world," it was primarily as spectators who knew that they would soon return to their comfortable homes in America and continue with their assured paths to academic and financial success.

I know a family with two teen-age sons who attended the finest preparatory schools and universities. The family lived at the edge of an ethnically diverse neighborhood, but in an upscale house that did not resemble the others in the neighborhood. The two young men were reticent to venture into the central part of town for fear of encountering people of color, who they feared and considered inferior.

This anecdote sadly exemplifies America's elite. What they do share is the ideology of Progressivism. In *Coming Apart,* Murray addresses the growing reality of a distinct intellectual and socioeconomic class in America, with increasing stratification of American society based on intelligence and socioeconomic privilege (C. Murray, 2012). The chances for a non-elite young person competing effectively to achieve the American dream are being lost.

The story goes like this: Intelligent obsessional men and women meet on elite university campuses, or at prestigious graduate schools, or later in life at prestigious firms. They work together as doctors, lawyers, or in the financial sector. They date, marry, and have children — but not so many as to interfere with their careers. They are economically well to do, sometimes exceptionally so.

To the extent that genetic and environmental factors contribute and their family situation is relatively stable, their children are likely to exhibit levels of intelligence and obsessionality equal to or greater than their parents. They will be schooled, live in the same upscale neighborhoods, and assume power in society at the corporate, academic, and political levels. They will be encapsulated; they will live out of touch with others other than those in their circle and they will tend to share similar values and be less accepting, and even incredulous, concerning differences of opinion. There has always been privilege in society. But, in America, there used to be places where the mixing of those from different strata of society would occur, be it in public schools, playgrounds, or in the armed services. This is no longer the case.

The obsessional elite learn from an early age that intelligence is important. Often intellectually gifted, they view those of lesser intelligence as inferior. I attended a New York City public high school in the 1960s that was selecting young students for their aptitude in science to counter the advances being made post-Sputnik in the then-Soviet Union. The students were chosen for their intelligence, and they were encouraged to study with a focus on the sciences in classrooms apart from others of their grade level. I was selected to be part of this elite student body but had many friends who were not, and continued to befriend them. I recall being angered at the attitudes expressed by my new fellow "elite" students toward those who were not intellectually gifted. They dismissed them contemptuously as "dumb" and "ill-bred." It was an experience I will never forget, and this was in a New York City public school, not an elite private school!

Indoctrinated into today's Progressivism, the elite learn that it is "good" to champion the causes of the disadvantaged, but they will rarely encounter them directly or ever know how they live. That is unimportant to them; what apparently matters is that they be seen to be on the "right" side of the issue.[48] They never consider that they might be harming the objects of their sympathy, as they are viewed as "symbols," rather than as real people.

Some of these elite young people will enter academics and become scholars. Sowell restricts this moniker to those who advance *ideas* as the major part of their profession. This includes those in academia, but it excludes physicians, lawyers, engineers, etc., whose ideas largely translate into purposeful action. The obsessional style of the intellectual is evidenced by the certainty they hold concerning the correctness of their positions. An example of the shared mentality of these intellectuals was exhibited in a mass e-mailing that I received from the president of the university. Universities often include the College, Law School, Medical School, etc. In the e-mail, the vetting procedures suggested by the Trump administration for countries known to be breeding grounds for Islamic terrorism were openly attacked. Following an initial expression of dismay and anxiety concerning the Executive Order, it said:

> I have focused this letter on just a few of the issues and challenges brought to the fore by Friday's executive order and related developments…and in an effort to redress inequality, in seeking ways for people with starkly different views to speak and to listen across widening divides, and in striving for a shared commitment to the truth. These and other present concerns are anything but endnotes; they lie at the core of our university.

The content and tone of her message included no consideration that there might be faculty members who did not share these Progressive views, as they have become the dogma of the institution. This assumed

---

48 This recalls the issues encountered by George H.W. Bush's failure to have a clue as to how much a container of milk cost when running unsuccessfully for a 2nd term as president in 1992 or Hillary Clinton's carrying around a sample of hot sauce when visiting the African-American communities of the South.

homogeneity of thought by Progressive intellectuals stigmatizes those who do not share their *weltanschauung,* and undermines what was the traditional liberal position of academia. But those days are over.

Progressive higher education in this country has become a place where rigid ideology has replaced the marketplace of diverse ideas. University professors inject their own political views into the classroom, limit free speech by espousing "politically correct" notions, and punish those who, with genuinely reasoned arguments and ardor, disagree with Progressive ideology.

In recent years, the situation has only worsened. Activist college teachers encourage students to protest and even to riot. The course curricula are riddled with nonsensical courses that promote the notion of America as an evil and systemically racist country. Some of these institutions have huge endowments, while claiming to be "non-profits," so that they can benefit from federal tax exemptions. Unfortunately, their financial support often comes from the government and from alumni who have failed to recognize that "This is not your father's 'Harvard, Princeton, or Yale'." President Trump's plan to defund these universities was a first step in the right direction. Unless efforts are made to address this problem, defunding these institutions and reviewing the curricula of teachers who are preaching radicalism, America may never recover from their malignant influence.

We are witnessing a progressive divide in America based on educational opportunities, socioeconomic status, and political views. There is an obsessional elite emerging that is positioned to determine the future of all Americans. The greatest threat to a democratic republic is the emergence of an oligarchy whose influence is unchallenged. This is occurring in America today, and it must be recognized and somehow discouraged.

Chapter 10: Political Correctness

Political correctness does not legislate tolerance; it only organizes hatred.

— Jacques Barzun

I believe that political correctness can be a form of linguistic fascism and it sends shivers down the spine of my generation who went to war against fascism.

— P.D. James

In a gradual process that began in the 1960s, the United States and much of Western Europe has embraced the behavioral strategy of "political correctness." Political correctness aims at not offending any individual or group in society that is perceived as potentially disadvantaged. However, it limits this to people of color, the poor, women, the LGBT community, and religious minorities that Progressive ideology currently judges as persecuted. Other minorities, e.g., Asian-Americans or Jews in America, are not included in this category, nor are Christian minorities in the Islamic world who are persecuted regularly, because they do not fit into the Progressive narrative. What political correctness ultimately aims at is to control the ideas and speech approved by a Progressive state.

Although the idea has roots in the sensibilities of the Hebrew prophets and the ethical standards of compassionate Christianity, political correctness outstrips the Biblical message, taking it to extremes the prophets would not have sanctioned. The Biblical prophets were charged with confronting a corrupt ruling class with unpleasant truths, a position antithetical to political correctness, which ignores or seeks to deny truths that shed a negative light on Progressivism, and instead seeks to quash resistance via intimidation.

The term *politically correct* emerged into the language and culture of America in the late 20th CE. It was first recorded in William Safire's *Political Dictionary* (Safire, 2008). It became part of the American public debate in the late 1980s, and the media's use of the term was widespread by the 1990s. Political correctness was the label applied to a range of policies in academia, including supporting affirmative action and sanctions against anti-minority speech. A stated goal of political correctness is to revise the traditional academic curricula to reflect the growing emphasis on diversity and identity politics, a trend fostered by the conflation of feminism, gay rights, and racial power politics.

In the journal *American Speech*, Edna Andrews notes that the goal of culturally inclusive and gender-neutral language is based on the concept that "language represents thought," and therefore can be discretely applied to control thought (Andrews, 1996). Janet B. Parks and Mary Ann Robinson validated Andrews' opinion that the language-thought relationship supports the "reasonable deduction...[of] cultural change via linguistic change" with respect to gender role (Parks & Robertson, 2000). Advocates of "culturally inclusive" language and "gender-neutral" language proposed that such locutions were not optional but mandatory.

The Social Construction of Reality, the seminal text by sociologists Berger and Luckmann, played an important role in contributing to the development of political correctness (Berger & Luckmann). They argued that both subjective and objective realities are influenced by perspective and as such by both imagined and real events. This is an extension of Aaron Beck's cognitive-behavioral theory, in which perspectives are restructured by cognitions and speech (Beck, 1979).

Political correctness fosters agendas that are not necessarily supported by evidence. "Facts" are declared, rather than proven; challenges are met with resistance and hostile epithets. The moral superiority of politically correct ideas is assumed as beyond question by those who promote it. Political correctness insists that there is no difference between men and women, blacks and whites, those who are intellectually capable and those who are not. Yet intellectual and biological differences between races have been recognized objectively for years. Most have shown that on average African-Americans score lower on measures of IQ as a group than Caucasians and Asians. In the *Bell Curve*, Herrnstein and Murray argued that human intelligence is influenced by inherited and environmental factors and are the best predictor of future success (Herrnstein & Murray, 1994). Despite abundant objective evidence, these authors have for years been subjected to withering criticisms in the lay and academic press by politically correct advocates who refuse to accept uncomfortable facts that do not support their ideology (C. Murray, 2020).

But these same critics would not dream of questioning why the winners of running marathons are virtually always Africans, or deny that much of American sport is currently dominated by elite black athletes. They refuse to accept that trans-gender "females" have a distinct biological advantage over girls who play sports. For reasons that only the politically correct obsessional mind can fathom, reverse biological bias or social discrimination is acceptable and justified because it does not disturb the underlying ideological dogma.

The refusal to accept differences when they suggest that racial minorities are on average at a *real* disadvantage intellectually through no fault other than circumstances beyond their control, is part of an obsessional strategy that compulsively insists on equalizing differences. Politically correct ideas are configured by the nexus of neurotic guilt for even suggesting that there are individuals who cannot keep up through no fault of their own, and the will to control the behavior of others by censoring their ability to make critical comments, even when factually correct.

But it is doubtful that biological or cultural differences can be erased by well-meaning concerns, early education, or federal financial assistance. There are some things that money cannot buy. Does this then mean that America should give up on those who cannot achieve at the level of others? Absolutely not, but it does suggest that realistically designed educational programs should be offered to young people, rather than trying to fit a square peg into a round hole, or by holding back those young people who may be intellectually gifted (C. Murray, 2008). This is the real meaning of diversity.

The Progressive program of political correctness can be likened to the Hans Christian Anderson story of the "Emperor's New Clothes." There are a host of collective illusions currently blinding society to the truth, based on magical thinking, illusions, and collective fear. Real differences between the sexes or races are perceived by Progressives primarily in terms of power and, as it is their goal to wrest power from Conservative white men, political correctness must deny the realities of difference. Despite this disingenuous perspective, and its enormous unpopularity among "non-believers," the politically correct movement has made great strides in society, and particularly in Progressive institutions, by intimidation. It has created a self-serving bureaucracy whose role is to disseminate politically correct doctrine and to insure its application and enforcement. Anyone who has ever been sent to "HR" for "sensitivity training" can attest to this.

The politically correct movement would force Americans to believe that words are dangerous — that they irreparably injure others, that they make "racists" and "bigots" of us all — unless we strictly censor them. Sensitivity training has become a routine topic of paramount importance in many of America's institutions. Whereas increased sensitivity is not a bad idea, when carried to extremes and enforced with punitive actions directed against those whose speech is not judged as sufficiently "politically correct," one must question whether the First Amendment of the U.S. Constitution is being routinely violated.

In the hospital I worked in, physicians are compelled to take and pass frequent computerized training and exams based on slide show mini-seminars created by the hospital administration. The test questions are specifically designed to promote a politically correct agenda. The following is an actual multiple-choice question from a recent "exam."

Question: A patient stops you in the hall to ask directions. You should:

A. Walk by him because you are in a hurry
B. Stop to give him directions and then go on to your appointment
C. Direct him to the information booth in the lobby for assistance
D. Stop whatever you are doing and walk him to his destination

I guessed "B," but if you guessed that the correct answer is "D," you are on your way to being a politically correct superstar. Hopefully, not everyone is, at least not yet. It apparently doesn't matter to the hospital bureaucracy that a physician might have a clinic full of patients waiting for him, or that she is needed in the emergency room, or that he might have to perform a critical surgical procedure scheduled in the next five minutes. No, all of this is of secondary importance. Instead, walking a patient across the hospital to deliver him in person is the greatest concern. The take home message: a good physician is a caring physician. Or perhaps more accurately, the good physician is a "virtue signaling" physician!

I missed the correct answer because I couldn't believe it. Frankly, I did not practice medicine for 40 years to assume my newly prescribed role as a hospital guide to meet the inane goals of the Progressive agenda. Many of my colleagues laughed at this question, but few took it seriously enough to question who was now running the hospital. Like "good" compliant obsessionals, they gave the expected answer and continued about their business. This is what enables the outrageous fringe of Progressivism to succeed. Enabling it is never the correct answer.

WHAT'S IN A NAME?

New and ever-changing terminologies are routinely adopted by the politically correct to expunge potentially discriminatory implications. As Horowitz notes, "Negroes" became "Blacks," then "African-Americans," and now "People of Color" (Horowitz, 2016). But have they somehow changed? The answer is *no* and, as the ancient Buddhist saying goes, "the finger that points at the moon is not the moon." In short, changing a name does not change the thing itself. Those previously "crippled" are now "physically challenged," dwarves are "little people," and the list grows longer and ever-changing. Once a new term is introduced, the older term of speech is re-classified as "hate speech." This has led to a limited backlash from the right, and "political correctness" has become a label for ideas rejected by the political conservatives. President George W. Bush warned against a Progressive movement that would declare certain topics, expressions, even gestures, "off-limits." A blog by Conservative commentator Ed Kilgore in August of 2015 notes:

> The new era of liberal political correctness — in which colleges designate "free speech zones," words like "American" and "mother" are considered discriminatory, and children are suspended from school for firing make-believe weapons — has reached critical mass.

Even the Progressive-in-Chief Barack Obama criticized the extremity of political correctness on September 14, 2014:

> One thing I do want to point out is it's not just sometimes folks who are mad that colleges are too liberal that have a problem — sometimes there are folks on college campuses who are liberal, and maybe even agree with me on a bunch of issues, who sometimes aren't listening to the other side, and that's a problem, too. I was just talking to a friend of mine about this. You know, I've heard some college campuses where they don't want to have a guest speaker who is too conservative or they don't want to read a book if it has language that is offensive to African-Americans or somehow sends a demeaning signal towards women, and I gotta tell you, I don't agree with that either. I don't agree that you, when you become students at colleges, have to be coddled and protected from different points of view. Anybody who comes to speak to you and you disagree with, you should have an argument with them, but you shouldn't silence them by saying you can't come because I'm too sensitive to hear what you have to say. That's not the way we learn either.

Profound changes in how language is applied can change how individuals think about their environment and how they construe their surroundings. But establishing an expurgated common language in society damages freedom of expression. This situation was imagined by a prescient George Orwell, who described a totalitarian future in which there would be ever-changing dictionaries of socially acceptable "Newspeak" (Orwell, 1950).

There is a tremendous fear of social rejection that people feel when disapproved of, and this is especially true in today's obsessional society. Those who refuse to accept political correctness can expect to be shunned, ostracized, and risk losing their jobs in today's America; *that* is real, and unacceptable. The academics who fostered these notions have, in some cases, fallen victim to how their own ideas have been applied. As Berger recently noted (Berger, 2011):

The cultural situation in America today (and indeed in all Western societies) is determined by the cultural earthquake of the nineteen-sixties, the consequences of which are very much in evidence. What began as a counter-culture only some thirty years ago has achieved dominance in elite culture and, from the bastions of the latter (in the educational system, the media, the higher reaches of the law, and key positions within government bureaucracy), has penetrated both popular culture and the corporate world. It is characterized by an amalgam of both sentiments and beliefs that cannot be easily catalogued, though terms like 'progressive,' 'emancipators' or 'liberationist' serve to describe it. Intellectually, this new culture is legitimated by a number of loosely connected ideologies — leftover Marxism, feminism and other sexual identity doctrines, racial and ethnic separatism, various brands of therapeutic gospels, and of environmentalism. An underlying theme is antagonism toward Western culture in general and American culture in particular.

A prevailing spirit is one of intolerance and a grim orthodoxy, precisely caught in the phrase "political correctness" (Berger, *Adventures,* p. 34).

Unwittingly, academics like Berger have witnessed how the extreme application of their ideas has led to "grim" results. Burdened by an unremitting perfectionist morality and harsh super-ego that is unable "to take a joke," humorless political correctness parallels the anhedonia of the obsessional. It is a Puritanical totalitarian mindset that should be anathema in American society. But as this mode of censorship has been adopted by a wide swath of Americans, it is currently questionable to what extent its effects can now be reversed.

The intolerance expressed by those who espouse politically correct values is extreme. An example of their hypocrisy was evident in the 2016 presidential election. During the 2016 presidential debates between Donald Trump and Hillary Clinton, Trump was queried by Fox News moderator Chris Wallace as to whether he would accept the results of the November election if he were to lose. Trump refused to answer definitively, suggesting that it would depend on circumstances, claiming that he had reasons to question whether there might be irregularities at the voting booths. This response, reasonable to most, evoked a hurricane of criticism by the Progressive left, who attacked Trump for questioning the democratic principles that America was founded upon.

But when Trump unexpectedly won the election, these same critics questioned whether the election results were valid and insisted on exploring recounts in several states Trump won by wide margins. When those revealed no substantive irregularities, blame was then cast on interference in the election process by the FBI and on the Russian government. Rioting occurred in several major cities and protestors vowed to resist any efforts that opposed their politically correct agenda, regardless of the will of the American electorate.

When Trump apparently lost the 2020 election and his supporters dared to question the results, they were condemned, deplatformed from social media, and labeled as seditionists. The double-standard is mind blowing.

The inability of some Progressives to confront truths may speak to their naiveté with respect to wielding power, as Emma Jung noted (E. Jung, 1985). Both women and minorities have had little experience with power, with how the political process works, or with how power periodically changes hands. It is no great surprise that, having felt that they were getting closer to achieving their Progressive goals under the leadership of Barack Obama and Hillary Clinton, the reactions of Progressives to Trump's election in 2016 was extreme and irrational.

One might readily dismiss political correctness as nonsense if it were not for the power that has accrued to those who insist on it. This same strategy was, and is still, used in totalitarian countries, including China and North Korea, to control their populations. But is this what America or Western Europe *really* want for their futures? And, if not, what is keeping the leaders of America from directly confronting and denouncing this approach? This country went through a similar situation in the McCarthy era in the 1950s, where people were indiscriminately labeled "Communists" and their lives were ruined. There are high-ranking individuals who have spoken out against the harm that political correctness is doing, but why is it not being actively confronted before it undermines the future of the Western world? The unfortunate answer is that it serves the psychological and economic interests of a hypersensitive obsessional globalist elite who cannot truly comprehend where their narcissism is leading America.

CHAPTER 11: RADICAL ISLAMIC TERRORISM

And kill them wherever you find them and turn them out
from where they have turned you out. Fitnah is worse than
killing.... And fight them until there is no more disbelief.

— Quran 2:191-193

On the evening of Friday, November 13, 2015, terrorists armed with automatic weapons and suicide explosive belts attacked the city of Paris. A handful of men affiliated with the Islamic State (ISIS), whose stated goal is to restore the defunct Islamic caliphate and destroy Western secular civilization, murdered and maimed more than 300 civilian Parisians before being killed or captured by police. This was the culmination of a string of recent terrorist attacks that included the destruction of a Russian passenger plane and the detonation of explosive devices in Lebanon and Turkey that killed innocent bystander several weeks before the incident in Paris. Additional terrorist attacks have transpired in America and most recently in Manchester and London, England. It is estimated that there are currently approximately 20,000 potential Islamic *jihadists* currently living in England and perhaps an even larger number in Europe.

An element within Islam has officially declared holy war, or *jihad*, on the secular West. This is not a group of criminals bent on financial success; it is a group of fundamentalist Islamists who are following a strict interpretation of the *Quran*. The socioeconomic and educational backgrounds of the terrorists belie claims of Progressives that their actions are best attributed to disaffected Muslim youth whose culture has not kept pace with the technological progress of the West. With typical Progressive denial of the truth, they would prefer to imagine that programs designed to, as usual, improve the socioeconomic status of the terrorist would cure the terrorist problem. Others are of the mindset that, if young Muslims could only partake in the opportunities offered by the secular West, then they would rapidly forget about terrorism and convert to Western consumerism. These attitudes confirm the ignorance of secular Progressives with respect to the power of deeply held religious beliefs. Indeed, many of the Islamic terrorist leaders have lived or been educated in the West and it has been their disgust, not envy, of what they see as rampant immorality that has led them to declare war on the West.

In virtually all cases of Islamic terrorism. one encounters a fundamentalist orthodox interpretation of the *Quran* that instructs Muslims to wage war on non-believers and to annihilate them without mercy. Islamic extremists believe that the West, led by America, has turned into a Godless hedonistic civilization that opposes the tenets of Islam:

> The Islamic State claimed responsibility on Saturday for the catastrophic attacks in the French capital, calling them "the first of the storm" and mocking France as a "capital of prostitution and obscenity" *(New York Times,* November 14, 2015).

> An unbiased student of religion will recognize that a war directed against the non-Islamic world that raged from the 7th until the 16th CE has been rekindled by those who wish to insti-

tute a theocratic Islamic caliphate. The fundamentalist Islamic jihadists who are waging this war have every intention of winning it, and they share a mindset that admits for neither negotiation nor compromise.

Unfortunately, this perspective is beyond the understanding of most within the 21st CE secular Western world, especially the Progressive intellectual elite who are ignorant of Islam. It appears to be beyond the ken of Progressives that there might be people who hate them precisely for the ideological agenda they support. They are naïve in their belief that supporting "good" Muslims will have any positive effect on radical Islamic terrorism, or in choosing to believe that military jihadism is not actually a part of Islam. Unfortunately, it is an ideology, that, like Nazism, must be eradicated if Western civilization is to prevail.

Political and religious turbulence in the Middle East has also set in motion the largest migration in history from Islamic countries to Europe. Europe, which traditionally opposed the influx of Islam, has, with the notable exception of several small Orthodox Christian countries in Eastern Europe, has now opened its doors wide to hundreds of thousands of immigrants who share little culturally in common with their new hosts. Nor has a proper vetting process been put into place that might identify whether these immigrants represent a security risk to their adopted countries.

Germany, the nation with unquestionably the worst record in history when it comes to respecting the rights of "others," has proudly led the way in accepting these immigrants, thereby irrevocably changing the cultural fabric of its country. Prime Minister Angela Merkel has argued that Germany must adopt a politically correct "face" as a lesson to the outside world that the new Germany has divested itself fully of its tainted past with respect to the Holocaust. But the Holocaust is over and the lives of its victims cannot be redeemed by opening Germany's boundaries to immigrants and undoubtedly an unknown number of lethal terrorists.

Indeed, it is an example of how little empathy Prime Minister Merkel's obsessional mind has in comparing these two situations. Germany murdered its own Jewish citizens, as well as Jews throughout Europe. Germany cannot atone for its enormous sins by ignoring the real threats posed by a horde of unvetted Muslim immigrants. As a consequence of this attack of conscience, it is very likely that Germany will become a haven for the launching of terrorist attacks directed against Germany and other countries in the West, and possibly Jewish targets, as was the case in Mumbai. Islamic terrorists murdered 3,000 American civilians in their destruction of the Twin Towers on 9/11/2001. Perhaps Prime Minister Merkel should consider the legacy of Germany if it proves to be responsible for even more innocent deaths in the 21st CE. One is meant to learn from history, not to obsessionally attempt to undo it.

A World Without Borders

The administration of Barack Obama, in addition to expressing a desire to allow large numbers of unvetted immigrants from terrorist-torn Syria, allowed the persistent immigration of illegal aliens across its southern border. The number of illegal immigrants from Central and South America in the U.S. reached record highs over the eight years of the Obama administration. Border agents were ordered to stand down or in many cases to capture and then immediately release illegal aliens. There was little effective border control, as illegal aliens, including criminals and drug traffickers, moved back and forth from Mexico into the U.S.

Donald Trump, recognizing the profound dangers of porous borders, fought for and succeeded in building several hundred miles of security wall along the southern border and made efforts to enforce the law with respect to the expulsion of criminal illegal aliens. On his first day in office, President Biden made it his priority to rescind law enforcement at the border and the construction of the border wall. The result of this policy promises to be devastating to the health and economic well-being of the average American. However, it will likely benefit selfish large corporations looking for an ever-cheaper work force, and the Democratic Party that seeks to expand its voting base so as to never have to be challenged seriously again in future elections.

As historian Samuel Huntington argued, the demographics of America have changed with extraordinary speed since the 1960s, when quotas related to Asian and Hispanic immigration were all but abolished (Huntington, 2005).

Pluralism is a long-standing ideal of American society but one that inevitably also called for the assimilation of core American values. But for Progressives today, pluralism is a means for achieving a utopian humanism that does not simply welcome the notion of difference but insists upon it. The fact is that America has never been a true "melting pot." It has allowed people of different racial, ethnic, and religious backgrounds to co-exist with persistent degrees of ethnic tension. Some groups have never fully integrated into society, as they tend to prefer the company of those who share their own cultural, ethnic, and religious particularities.

For Progressives, the realities of difference have given way to ideological abstractions. To the extent that genuine difference and ethnic tensions undermine the myth of egalitarianism, they are denied. The anger that Progressives exhibit toward those who provide evidence to suggest that diversity and identity politics may actually undermine American unity belies the intolerance of political correctness (Horowitz, 2004).

CONCLUSION

Having argued for the parallels between obsessionality and today's Progressivism, it is necessary to explain why the latter in recent times has adopted extreme positions. Many have already been touched upon, and have been with us for many decades. But what *is* new and rapidly changing are the digital technologies that have profoundly changed how we live and how we communicate. The Internet, smart phones, and social networking have all served to disseminate ideas, and social networking has increased psychological pressures for many to yield to collective thought, what has been pejoratively referred to as "groupthink."

Freud and Jung both expressed a distinct aversion to the psychology of groups. They recognized that autonomy was invariably undermined in groups because man, as a social animal, is suggestible and easily influenced by his peers. Communications in groups are complex and include both explicit and implicit elements. Indeed, individuals in groups tend to "synchronize" around certain modes of thought, feelings, and behaviors (C.G. Jung, 1984). This "participation mystique" promotes shared ideas and actions, and is commonly seen in traditional societies. The psychoanalytical movement of the early 20th CE was aimed specifically at fostering individual autonomy and reducing conformity.

Furthermore, people in groups are prone to unstable and irrational behaviors. As Jung said, "Masses are always breeding grounds for psychic epidemics" (C.G. Jung, 1928). Recent times have seen "spontaneous demonstrations," some violent, rapidly organized through social media. This was the organizing medium for the "Arab spring" demonstrations and, more recently, in reaction to the 2016 American presidential election results.

There are enormous numbers of people spending large amounts of time on Facebook and other social media (Asano, 2017):

> The amount of time people spend on social media is constantly increasing. Teens now spend up to nine hours a day on social platforms, while 30% of all time spent online is now allocated to social media interaction. And the majority of that time is on mobile — 60% of social media time spent is facilitated by a mobile device.

This is quickly becoming the primary modality for communicating with others, and many users also get their news from it. Whether information is coming from mainstream or digital news networks, they are likely to show bias toward Progressive ideologies, largely because those in the digital communications industry and the so-called "tekkies" virtually uniformly hold these views. The Internet is, in many respects, the best example of the unconstrained vision, in the sense that it resists any sort of regulation or censorship. But, paradoxically, ideas offered through digital media are constrained by peer pressures.

The genius of a Mark Zuckerberg, the founder of Facebook, the largest social media network, was in recognizing peoples' yearning for connection in this modern age of uncertainty. People fear being isolated and worry about being socially rejected. For obsessionals, their ambivalence concerning intimate relationships makes social media an ideal mode of communication. Online, one can remain constantly in touch with "friends" without having to interact with them in person. A patient described her experience with dating on social media:

> I've met large numbers of men online. I've spent hours messaging with some of them. I enjoy the banter, but I rarely choose to meet with them in person. When I do, I am invariably disappointed. They rarely meet my standards and, to be honest, I don't always meet theirs either. But I continue to spend hours "dating" online. It's better than feeling alone.

This vignette characterizes obsessional relationships in the 21st CE. Of course, people still meet in person, marry, and raise families. But, for many, social interactions are largely limited to Facebook and Twitter, due to their own perfectionism and fears of physical contact and sexually transmissible diseases.

Social media allows you to have an unlimited number of "friends" who are constantly evaluating what they like and don't like about what you are doing or who you claim to be. The social pressure to conform in this "unconstrained" system is enormous.

The 2016 presidential election proved how powerful these forces are. It was a widely shared "fact," according to polls taken prior to the election as well as in "exit polls" after the voting, that Donald Trump had "no path" to electoral college victory. This was repeated over and over by pollsters and by political commentators on mainstream media.

However, ardent Trump supporters continued to suggest that the overwhelming enthusiasm that they had witnessed at rallies for their candidate across the country did not jibe with the polls. When Trump finally won the electoral vote by a wide margin, the pollsters were forced to admit they had been wrong. The reasons varied; perhaps they had not sampled a representative audience due to the widespread use of cell phones, etc. But one point kept re-emerging in their analysis, and that was that individuals who supported Trump were reluctant to admit it in public due to fears of being rejected by "friends" in person or on social media. A woman patient who lives in Boston put it to me like this:

> I'm sick of the political correctness and the identity politics. I don't want to share my bathroom with transsexual men. But I keep my mouth shut because all my friends despise Trump and I don't want to be labeled a "bigot" or a "racist" by them, so I say nothing. But I can't wait to vote and I've got my fingers crossed. I'm sick of Obama and his Progressive ideologies, and I don't think that I'm alone. He may even win despite what everyone says.

We may never know for certain what "fooled" the pollsters in the 2016 election, but the above phenomenon was apparently widespread. The social pressures induced by the desire not to be rejected by others, to be a "nice" person, and to avoid confrontation, all contributed to a quasi-involuntary muteness by many who held political views that did not conform with those on mainstream and social media networks.

But the most widely shared ideas are those created by the mass media, including movies, the music industry, and network news, virtually all of which share Progressive values. Hollywood and music industry luminaries have taken it upon themselves to speak up, at times stridently, against Trump and the constrained vision of Conservative

Republicans. But, with rare exceptions, these "stars" are no more qualified than the average individual to evaluate socio-political issues, although they do take advantage of fame to assume the bully pulpit. It is difficult to ascertain to what extent their message is influential. By all indications based on the 2016 election, it may be highly overrated, but it certainly plays well when preaching to the choir.

Celebrities in politics is a relatively new phenomenon in American society. Indeed, many prominent political figures, including Donald Trump, Arnold Schwarzenegger, and Al Franken, come from the world of show business where their reputations preceded them. However, Trump is not only a reality TV star; he is also a genuinely successful businessman who brought his experience to the presidency.

Perhaps the greatest unifying force in modern society, particularly among young people, is music. More people listen to music, and more of the time, than ever before. The influence of the Beatles and the pop revolution of the 1960s on the non-conforming attitudes of world youth should not be underestimated. The widespread availability of shared music over the Internet has become a way of bonding for young people and, for many, it is the most important aspect of their lives. The messages that are conveyed by modern music are varied. The values of hip-hop music are certainly different than those conveyed by country music, and their audiences are largely distinct. Their relative popularities track with the divergent visions of their listeners.

There is an antinomic perspective and one of universalism that is conveyed through the lyrics and culture of modern rock music. John Lennon recognized the influence that music had on his audience when he made the controversial statement that "The Beatles are bigger than Jesus Christ." Progressive rock often seeks to undermine conservative values and it has potentially been the greatest factor in doing so. The late John Lennon's lyrics to the song, "Imagine," sums up the attitude:

Imagine there's no heaven
It's easy if you try
No hell below us
Above us only sky
Imagine all the people
Living for today…

You may say I'm a dreamer
But I'm not the only one
I hope someday you'll join us
And the world will be as one.

— "Imagine" (from "Imagine: John Lennon" soundtrack)

This a secularized description of a global peaceful utopia. Lennon acknowledged this, and it is the vision of Progressives today. There has been a recent campaign to replace the "Star Spangled Banner" with Lennon's "Imagine" as the new American national anthem. These ideas are not being read in books: instead, they are heard repeatedly on digital media and undoubtedly have much to do with the social, religious, and political views currently professed by Progressives.

Yet it is worth noting that the politically correct movement turns a blind eye to the overtly violent and demeaning lyrics of hip-hop music. These lyrics, which routinely include the "N" word, refer to violent sexual behavior, are misogynistic, and encourage violence directed against authority, are enthusiastically adopted by the same Progressives who would immediately decry the same lyrics if offered by a white man. The hypocrisy of this stance is palpable but never addressed by Progressives as, from their perspective, non-Whites have license to say whatever they please without criticism and to promote violent tendencies in their songs without it being labeled "hate speech." Indeed, when actual violence has erupted on campuses and the inner cities, one is hard pressed to find a major political figure on the Progressive left who opposes it, although some will pay lip service to its inappropriateness if forced to respond.

While it is possible to conclude that Progressives are all hypocritical, manipulative liars, it is likely as accurate that they hold a "sacred" vision that cannot be challenged. Indeed, failed attempts at dialogue resemble what occurs when attempting to introduce an opposing idea to religious fundamentalists, who can brook no exceptions to their beliefs, be they objectively true or not.

In this regard, Progressivism closely resembles a fundamentalist "religion" that has replaced traditional religion. They view the latter as irrational, yet their chosen ideology is no less so. Psychoanalysts routinely see how individuals tend to replace old bad habits with new ones without recognizing that no fundamental change has transpired. What has not changed is the obsessionality that often drives these beliefs.

As Jung noted (C.G. Jung, 1962):

Loss of roots and lack of tradition neuroticize the masses and prepare them for collective hysteria. Collective hysteria calls for collective therapy, which consists in abolition of liberty and terrorization. When rationalistic material holds sway, states tend to develop less into prisons than into lunatic asylums (Jung, para. 282).

Jung lived through the rise of Nazi fascism, but his observations ring true for what is occurring in America today. There has unquestionably been a loss of religious belief and traditional moral values in America. This has been accompanied by a culture of therapy, as Rieff refers to it (Rieff, 1966). As Jung terms it, "collective therapy" appears to be a driving force for politically correct ideology that, in turn, has limited individual freedoms and has led to periodic violent eruptions.

The obsessional defenses of an overwrought society are beginning to unravel in the face of opposing realities. The daily hysterical broadcasts concerning President Trump's activities are examples of this behavior and, frankly, they continue to undermine the future of America. Indeed, it is virtually impossible for Trump's opponents to define clearly what he has done wrong, but that does not appear to matter. In their last effort to discredit him, the House of Representatives voted to impeach him with one week left in his presidency, an example of their persistent spiteful mean-spiritedness. However, it would behoove those currently in power to force a conclusion to this interminable hysteria, lest the country end in ruin. A critical study of history might also help naïve Progressives to recognize that the path America is on today closely resembles that of the Soviet Union, Communist China, and Nazi Germany.

Obsessional Conservatives do not suffer from hysteria to the same degree as Progressives. This may be because they are more secure in their traditions and moral beliefs. The "Never Trumpers" are certainly not ideologically aligned with the left, but they were as narcissistically wounded by Trump's election and their current political irrelevance. Trump left Progressives insecure concerning what the future holds for them and with no secure container for their anxieties, violent reactions ensued.

Currently, political correctness and outright censorship are producing a reign of terror that will divide generations, racial groups, religious denominations, obsessionals from non-obsessionals, and paralyze America. The Progressive perspective is entrenched in America's educational system and in institutions of higher learning where the Western literary canon and historical facts are challenged and reinterpreted to expunge any hypersensitive perceived elements of bigotry, racism, or inequality. American history is being inaccurately re-visioned with the aim of emphasizing the historically minor contributions of people of color. Comparable strategies are routinely adopted in totalitarian societies.

I live in Boston, a city rich in early American history. I studied the American Revolution while in public school, and later again as an interested adult. When I recently visited Faneuil Hall, a public historic building dating back to the American Revolution, there were media screenings of re-enacted Revolutionary War history for tourists. But rather than recounting the rich history of the times, these films focused on the contributions of African Americans and women. Although both undoubtedly played a role in society at the time, with respect to that of white men it was objectively a minor one. The recent 1619 Project proposed by the N.Y. Times erroneously attempts to frame the founding of America around the issue of slavery. The Progressive goal is not to educate with facts; it is to praise and overvalue underclasses. They are not merely equal to the white man; they are clearly superior to him. That's the message. But revisionist history is a dangerous activity and leads to phenomena such as "Holocaust denial." Political correctness and phobic avoidance of anything that might offend undermines proper education by politicizing it. This is a strategy to impose a top-down control of the thought processes of others.

The politically correct movement exhibits both the positive and defensive elements of obsessionality. At the core of the politically correct movement is "rational" irrationality. It declares realities not supported by fact. It is dishonest. It fosters rigid defenses that brook no criticism. Its inability to withstand criticism belies its fragility.

In a statement to the press in August of 2015, Donald Trump boldly declared that "I don't, frankly, have time for total political correctness. And, to be honest with you, this country doesn't have time, either." Virtually all the Republican presidential candidates in the 2016 pre-election campaign identified political correctness as the major problem in America.

America was, in part, predicated on the adventurous spirit of the individual. It espoused fierce non-conformist entrepreneurial attitudes. Despite a credo of respect for others, differences were recognized and critically evaluated. There was an underlying sense of what was good for America and, when the country was wrong, cooperative efforts were generally made to correct its course of action.

America is a multicultural society; it used to be a confederation of like-minded citizens who espoused the shared values of the dominant society. As Huntington noted, there was an American ethos (Huntington, 2005). But if new immigrants fail to adopt it, one can expect profound changes in American values and in its world standing. Indeed, Barack Obama's America was well on its way to making America a declining power, both economically and strategically, in the world.

World-dominating nations come and go, and it is possible to iden-tify the factors that lead to their fall, as Gibbon argued in his magisterial opus on the *Decline and Fall of The Roman Empire* (Gibbon, 2010). Certainly, globalization will have a limiting effect on the nation state and on the supremacy of America. It is possible that Trump's plan to "Make America Great Again" may prove to be a merely temporary interruption in America's progressive decline. However, its decline may not be inevitable. Restoring national borders, individual autonomy, and emphasis on national success could potentially reverse self-defeating Progressive trends.

It is not a virtue to have rampant crime on the streets of a nation. It is not in the best interests of a society at war to allow immigrants from terrorist nations to enter its borders unvetted. The success of America is not fostered by having minorities tyrannize the majority, or by embracing collective guilt concerning matters like slavery that occurred hundreds of years ago. America's youth deserve an education that serves them not only economically but in terms of maintaining freedom of ideas and speech. The replacement of traditional religion by secular obsessional systems is not progress. Progressive ideology, as it currently manifests in America, is both neurotic and masochistic. It is neither kind nor compassionate. It simply represses truth and replaces harsh realities with utopian illusions.

During the 2016 presidential campaign, Democratic partisan Paul Begala made the following remark on the Progressive news network CNN:

Donald Trump's America is fearful. Afraid of crime, afraid of terrorism, afraid of immigrants. His (Trump's) America is angry. Angry about political correctness. Angry about international trade. Angry with President Obama. And very, very angry about Hillary Clinton's candidacy (Begala, July 26, 2016).

It is difficult to see how confronting problems is a failing but, from the perspective of the Progressive left, it is. Furthermore, the anger that this "dark" position evokes in Progressives is difficult to explain except when recognized as the result of obsessional defenses. The "dark" view is not a threat to society, as Progressives suggest; it is only a threat to their tenuous sense of security. Freud, who was accused of having a "dark view" of the world, argued that optimism was an illusion that denied the biological instinctual world and reality (S. Freud, 1930). He saw it as an expression of the obsessional neurosis of mankind.

America can ill afford to remain the highly polarized nation it has become. The obsessional defenses of Progressives will not correct the injury being done to America. How to correct this in the future is uncertain, but it is clear that "political correctness" has no place in a free society. It should be swept away as soon as possible. The unbiased enforcement of law must replace a strategy of censorship. Women and minorities must learn how to wield power in ways that do not disadvantage others. White men are not the enemy and should not have to tolerate being stigmatized unnecessarily. Parents should assume primary responsibility for the education of their children with respect to values, not the federal government. The primacy of the family, except in cases of extreme dysfunction, should be sacred; neither schools nor the federal government have the moral right to intervene to separate children from parents, physically or ideologically.

Access to the best higher education should be open to less than perfectly performing obsessional students. The latter are too isolated and frankly too insecure to function well in positions of responsibility. One does not need to be an extraordinary student to be an excellent doctor or a lawyer and, ultimately, common sense serves one best in most careers. Murray has advised young people to get out and see how others live; it is excellent advice (C. Murray, 2014).

One of the positive aspects of Trump's presidency was that he was not an "intellectual." His ideas are pragmatic and commonsensical, even if they frighten Progressives. Protecting the homeland, reducing stifling regulations, and improving the economy may have some downsides, but the upsides are all rooted in common sense and, if enacted, could "Make America Great Again." The recent gains of women and minorities are not threatened by Trump policies, but they may be placed in a more proper perspective with respect to the traditional goals that helped America succeed.

It should be recognized that obsessionals have a deep-seated fear of success and tend to create situations with unsuccessful outcomes. This is true of many intellectuals as well, and it well describes the Progressive agenda for America today. So perhaps the less than totally refined methods of a successful and egotistical businessman are exactly what the country currently requires. If the world can regain an element of stability via clear, direct action, it may quell the high levels of existential angst that drive obsessional ideation and inaction.

Progressives insist that claims that the 2020 election was "stolen" are seditious and that those who promote this opinion deserve to be punished. However, there is no doubt that the election *was* stolen, if not by actual fraud at the ballot box, by a Progressive media and social media elite that conspired together to keep the truth about President Trump's accomplishments and the problems with the Biden campaign away from American voters by suppressing and distorting the facts. A substantial percentage of Americans were never allowed to hear the truth about the President Trump's successes, nor the scandals that surrounded Biden and Kamala Harris and the radical Progressive policies that they intend to impose on an unwitting public. That *is* blatant election interference, and it should never be allowed to happen again in America.

Frankly, if history has taught us anything about extreme ideologies, it is that they cannot be reasoned with. The only way to deal with a misdirected ideology is to extinguish it so that it cannot re-emerge. This may sound harsh but, 70 years after the end of World War II, it is worth remembering that nothing stopped the Third Reich or Imperial Japan short of destruction. Americans need to be clear that the recalcitrant ideologies of fundamentalist Islam cannot be reasoned with, and unfortunately the same may be true for extreme Progressivism.

Until law, order, and sanity are restored in this country, the rantings of the left are certain to become increasingly hostile and difficult to contain. One must consider the possibility that their unconscious goal may be to destroy the social fabric of this country. All of the signs are there. We will not benefit from a French Revolution in 21st CE America. It is not a scenario that normal Americans should embrace.

Finally, the trend among Progressives to devalue their fellow Americans who hold different opinions should be reversed. There is a disturbing tendency among the Progressive elite to dehumanize their opposition. They apparently feel that those who hold opposing views are not qualified to determine the future of America. This is a dangerous, elitist mindset and exactly what the Founding Fathers hoped to avoid.

Trump's "Make America Great Again" movement will not go away. At least 74 million Americans voted for it and fervently support it. It will be hard for Progressives to govern and, if they do not recognize this, they may succeed in pushing America into a genuine civil war. As the unfortunate events at the nation's Capitol building on January 6, 2021 suggest, there are many Americans who have had enough of policies that benefit only part of the country.

As I have argued, the opposing visions in America have gender, racial, and cultural underpinnings. There are clearly economic issues at play as well, and these cannot be underestimated. But greed and corruption are themselves psychologically determined. The fact is that narcissistic and obsessional psychopathologies are driving the political divisiveness in America today. They must be addressed before it is too late.

References

Alinsky, S.D. (1971). *Rules for Radicals*. New York: Vintage Books.

Andrews, E. (1996). Cultural sensitivity and political correctness: The linguistic problem of naming. *American Speech, 71*, 389-404.

Arendt, H. (1976). *The Origins of Totalitarianism*. Orlando: Harvest.

Ariely, D. (2012). *The (Honest) Truth About Dishonesty*. New York: Harper Perennial.

Asano, E. (2017). *How Much Time Do People Spend on Social Media?* Association,

A.P. (1994). *Diagnostic and Statistical Manual of Mental Disorders: DSM-IV* (4th edn. ed.). Washington, DC: American Psychiatric Association.

Barrie, J. (1906). *Peter Pan of Kensington Gardens*. London: Hodder and Stoughton.

Beck, A. (1979). *Cognitive Therapy and the Emotional Disorders*. New York: Penguin.

Becker, E. (1973). *Denial of Death*. New York: Free Press.

Berger, P. (2011). *Adventures of an Accidental Sociologist*. Amherst: Prometheus Books.

Berger, P. & Luckmann, T. (1966). *The Social Construction of Reality: A Treatise in the Sociology of Knowledge*. New York: Open Road.

Bloom, A. (2012). *Closing of the American Mind*. New York: Simon & Schuster.

Bloom, A. (2016). *Republic of Plato*. New York: Basic Books.

Bowlby, J. (1969). *Attachment and Loss*. New York: Basic Books.

Cannon, W.B. (1932). *Wisdom of the Body*. New York: Norton.

Chapman, M. (2020). Trump: Pulitzer Prizes on Russia 'Collusion' Should Be Returned, 'They Were All Wrong.' CNS News, cnsnews.com, May 8, 2020.

Cohen, S.J.D. (2014). *Maccabees to Mishnah* (3rd ed.). Louisville: W. J. Knox.

D'Souza, D. (1991). *Illiberal Education*. New York: Free Press.

Damasio, A. (2000). *The Feeling of What Happens*. New York: Mariner.

Diagnostic and Statistical Manual of Mental Disorders-V. (2010). Washington, DC: American Psychiatric Society.

Dunn, J.D.G. (1991). *Parting of the Ways*. London: SCM.

Eco, U. (1990). *Travels in Hyperreality*. New York: Harvest Books.

Edelman, G. (1989). *The Remembered Present*. New York: Basic Books.

Ehrman, B. (2012). *Did Jesus Exist?* New York Harper One.

Ellis, J. (2015). *The Quartet*. New York: Vintage.

Erikson, E. (1995). *Young Man Luther: A Study in Psychoanalysis and History*. New York: W.W. Norton & Son.

Ferenzci, S. (1955). *Final Contributions to the Problems and Methods of Psychoanalysis*. London: Karnac.

Freud, A. (1992). *The Ego and the Mechanisms of Defense*. New York: Routledge.

Freud, S. (1907). Obsessive acts and religious practice. In J. Strachey (Ed.), *Standard Edition of the Complete Psychological Works of Sigmund Freud, Volume IX (1906-1908): Jensen's !Gradiva" and Other Works, 115-128* (Vol. IX, pp. 115-128). London: Hogarth Press.

Freud, S. (1923). Ego and the Id. In J. Strachey (Ed.), *Standard Edition*. London: Hogarth.

Freud, S. (1924). The Economic Problem of Masochism. In J. Strachey (Ed.), *Standard Edition of the Collected Works of Sigmund Freud* (Vol. 19, pp. 157-173). London: Hogarth Press.

Freud, S. (1927). Future of an Illusion. In J. Strachey (Ed.), *Standard Edition of the Complete Works of Sigmund Freud*. London: Hogarth Press.

Freud, S. (1930). Civilization and its Discontents. In J. Strachey (Ed.), *Standard Edition of the Collected Works of Sigmund Freud* (Vol. 21). London: Hogarth Press.

Freud, S. (1933). New Introductory Lectures. In J. Strachey (Ed.), *Standard Edition of the Collected Works of Sigmund Freud* (Vol. 22). London: Hogarth Press.

Freud, S. (1936). New Outline of Psychoanalysis. In J. Strachey (Ed.), *Standard Edition of the Collected Works of Sigmund Freud* (Vol. 22). London: Hogarth Press.

Freud, S. (1959). An Autobiographical Study: Inhibitions, Symptoms and Anxiety, The Question of Lay Analysis, and Other Works. In J. Strachey (Ed.), *Standard Edition of the Collected Works of Sigmund Freud* (Vol. 20). London: Hogarth Press.

Freud, S. (1959). Mourning and Melancholia. In J. Strachey (Ed.), *Standard Edition of the Collected Works of Sigmund Freud* (Vol. 14). London: Hogarth Press.

References

Freud, S. (1989). *Totem and Taboo* New York: W.W. Norton.

Fromm, E. (1960). *Escape from Freedom*. New York: Vintage.

Gelernter, D. (2007). *Americanism*. New York: Doubleday.

Gibbon, E. (2010). *Decline and Fall of the Roman Empire*. New York: Everyman's Library.

Gilligan, C. (1999). *In a Different Voice*. Cambridge: Harvard University Press.

Goddfried, J. & Shearer, E. (2016). News across social media platforms. *Pew Research Center*.

Goldberg, J. (2009). *Liberal fascism: the secret history of the American left, from Mussolini to the politics of change* (1st paperback ed.). New York: Broadway Books.

Gray, J. (2012). *Men are from Mars , Women are from Venus*. New York: Harper.

Habermas, J. (1981). *The Theory of Communicative Action*. Boston: Beacon Press.

Habermas, J. & Ratzinger, J. (2006). *The Dialectics of Secularization*. San Francisco: Ignatius.

Hall, C. (1999). *Primer of Freudian Psychology*. New York: Plume.

Hegel, G.W.F. (2016). *Elements of the Philosophy of the Right*. Cambridge: Cambridge University Press.

Herrnstein, R.J. & Murray, C. (1994). *The Bell Curve*. New York.

Holmes, K. (2016). *Closing of the Liberal Mind: How Groupthink and Intolerance Define the Left*. New York: Encounter Books.

Horowitz, D. (2004). *Unholy Alliance*. Washington, DC: Regnery Publishing.

Horowitz, D. (2016). *Progressive Racism*. New York: Encounter Books.

Horowitz, D. (2017). *Big Agenda*. New York: Humanix.

Hughes, G. (2010). *Political Correctness*. Chichester: John Wiley & Sons.

Huntington, S. (2005). *Who Are We?* New York: Simon & Schuster.

Ingram, I. (1961). Obsessional Illness in Mental Hospital Patients. *The British Journal of Psychiatry, 107*.

James, W. (2019). *Varieties of Religious Experience*. New York: Snova.

Janet, P. (1921). Fear of Action. *The Journal of Abnormal Psychology and Social Psychology*, Vol. 16, p. 150.

Jones, E. (1953). *Sigmund Freud: Life and Work*. London: Hogarth Press.

Jung, C.G. (1928). Development of Personality. In H. Read, M. Fordham & G. Adler (Eds.), *Collected Works of C.G. Jung* (Vol. 17). Princeton: Bollingen/ Princeton.

Jung, C.G. (1962). The Psychogenesis of Mental Disease. In H. Read, M. Fordham & G. Adler (Eds.), *Collected Works of C.G. Jung*. Princeton: Bollingen/ Princeton.

Jung, C.G. (1962). The Theory of Psychoanalysis. In H. Read, M. Fordham, G. Adler & W. McGuire (Eds.), *Collected Works of C.G. Jung* (Vol. 14). Princeton:Princeton/Bollingen.

Jung, C.G. (1972). *Psychological Types* (Vol. 6). Princeton: Bollingen Press.

Jung, C.G. (1984). *Psychology of Religion: West and East*. Princeton: Princeton University.

Jung, C.G. & Jaffe, A. (1989). *Memories, Dreams, Reflections*. New York: Vintage.

Jung, E. (1985). *Anima and Animus*. Dallas: Spring.

Kant, I. (1780). *Critique of Pure Reason*. London: Longmans, Green & Co.

Kernberg, O. (1995). *Borderline Conditions and Pathological Narcissism*. Northvale: Jason Aronson.

Keyes, R. (2016). *The Post-Truth Era: Dishonesty and Deception in Contemporary Life*. New York: St. Martin's Press.

Klein, M. (1958). Development of mental functioning. In F. Press (Ed.), *Envy and Gratitude: The Writings of Melanie Klein*. New York: Free Press.

Kohlberg, L. (1981). *Essays on Moral Development, Vol. I:* San Francisco: Harper & Row.

Kohut, H. (1971). *The Analysis of the Self: A Systematic Approach to the Psychoanalytical Treatment of Narcissistic Personality Disorders*. New York: International Universities Press.

Kradin, R. (1999). Generosity: a psychological and interpersonal motivational factor of therapeutic relevance. *J Anal Psychol, 44*(2), 221-236.

Kradin, R. (2007). Minding the Gaps: The Role of Informational Encapsulation and Mindful Attention in the Analysis of Transference. *Journal of Jungian Theory and Practice, 1*, 1-13.

Kradin, R. (2008). *The Placebo Response*. New York: Routledge.

Kradin, R. (2016). *Parting of the Ways*. New York: Academic Press.

Kradin, R. & Benson, H. (2000). Stress, the relaxation response and immunity. *Mod Asp Immunobiol, 1*, 110-113.

Kradin, R.L. (1997). The psychosomatic symptom and the self: a siren's song. *J Anal Psychol, 42*(3), 405-423.

Kradin, R.L. (2004). The placebo response: its putative role as a functional salutogenic mechanism of the central nervous system. *Perspect Biol Med, 47*(3), 328-338.

References

Kristol, I. (1995). *Neoconservatism: The Autobiography of an Idea*. New York: Simon & Schuster.

Lukianoff, G. and Haidt, J. (2015). The Coddling of the American Mind. The Atlantic, June, 2015 issue, cover story.

Lasch, C. (1979). *The Culture of Narcissism: American Life in an Age of Diminishing Expectations*. New York: W.W. Norton.

Lau, M. (2007). *A Comprehensive Commentary on Ethics of the Fathers*. New York: Mesorah.

Levenson, J. (1994). *Creation and the Persistence of Evil*. Princeton: Princeton/ Bollingen.

Maimonides. (2000). *Guide for the Perplexed*. New York: Dover.

Marx, K. & Engels, F. (2014). *The Communist Manifesto*. New York: International Publishers.

Mac Donald, H. (2016). *The Wars of Cops*. New York: Encounter Books.

Morris, N. (2016). How Do You Distinguish between Religious Fervor and Mental Illness? *Scientific American*.

Murray, C. (1984). *Losing Ground*. New York: Basic Books.

Murray, C. (1999). *The Underclass Revisited*. Washington, DC: AEI

Murray, C. (2008). *Real Education*. New York: Cox and Murray.

Murray, C. (2012). *Coming Apart*. New York: Crown Forum.

Murray, C. (2014). *Curmudgeon's Guide*. New York: Crown Business.

Murray, C. (2020). *Human Diversity*. New York: Twelve.

Neumayr, G. (2017). *The Political Pope*. New York: Center Street.

Neusner, J. & Chilton, B. (Eds.). (2009). *The Golden Rule*. Latham: University Press.

Nietsche, F. (2017). *The Essential Nietzsche: Beyond Good and Evil and The Genealogy of Morals*. London: Chartwell.

Nisbet, R. (1969). *Social Change and History*. Oxford: Oxford University Press.

Nugent, W. (2010). *Progressivism: A Very Short Introduction*. Oxford: Oxford.

Ogden, T. (2005). *Projection and Psychotherapeutic Technique*. London: Karnac.

Orwell, G. (1950). *1984*. New York: Penguin.

Parks, J.B. & Robertson, M.A. (2000). Development and Validation of an Instrument to Measure Attitudes Toward Sexist/Nonsexist Language. *Sex Roles, 42*, 415-438.

Piaget, J. (1960). *The Psychology of the Child*. New York: Basic Books.

Poll, G. (2016). Religion.

Prestigiacomo, A. (2016). Former Johns Hopkins psychiatrist blasts transgender movement. *The Wire.*

Psychological Healing: A Historical and Clinical Study. Vol. I. London: George Allen and Unwin. (1925).

Reich, W. (1980). *Character Analysis.* New York: Farrar Straus and Giroux.

Rich, J. (2010). *Modern Feminist Theory: An Introduction.* New York: Humanities-Ebooks.

Rieff, P. (1966). *Triumph of the Therapeutic.* Chicago: University of Chicago Press.

Rieff, P. (1979). *Freud: The Mind of the Moralist.* Chicago: University of Chicago.

Safire, W. (2008). *Political Dictionary.* Oxford: Oxford University Press

Salzman, L. (1977). *Treatment of the Obsessional Personality.* Northvale: Jason Aronson.

Sapolsky, R. (2017). *Behavior: The Biology of Humans at Our Best and Worst.* New York: Penguin Press.

Schama, S. (1990). *Citizens: A Chronicle of the French Revolution.* New York: Vintage.

Scholem, G. (1995). *The Messianic Idea in Judaism.* New York: Schocken.

Schwarz, H.S. (2003). *Revolt of the Primitive*: Transaction Publishers.

Shapiro, D. (1981). *Autonomy and Rigid Character.* New York: Basic Books.

Shoemaker, K. (2011). *Sanctuary and Crime in the Middle Ages.* New York: Fordham University Press, 284 pp.

Shorter, E. (1996). *From Fatigue to Paralysis.* New York: Free Press.

Sims, A. (2003). *Paul Ricouer.* London: Routledge.

Soloveichik, J. (2005). *Pesach, Sefirot and Shavuot.* New York: Lambda Publications.

Sowell, T. (2007). *A Conflict of Visions.* New York: Basic Books.

Sowell, T. (2011). *Intellectuals and Society.* New York: Basic Books.

Sowell, T. (2011). *The Thomas Sowell Reader.* New York: Basic Books.

Statistics, N.V. (2014). *National Marriage and Divorce Rate Trends 2000-2014.* Atlanta: U.S. Government

Steele, S. (2009). *White Guilt: How Blacks and Whites Together Destroyed the Promise of the Civil Rights Era.* New York: Harper Perennial.

Stern, D.N. (1985). *The Interpersonal World of the Infant.* New York: Basic Books.

Strozier, C. (2001). *Heinz Kohut: The Making of a Psychoanalyst.* New York: Farrar Straus and Giroux.

Sulloway, F. (1979). *Freud: Biologist of the Mind*. New York: Basic Books.

Sumption, J. (2000). *Albigensian Crusade*. New York: Faber and Faber.

Tomasello, M. (2016). *Natural History of Morality*. Cambridge: Harvard University Press.

Vermes, G. (2012). *Complete Dead Sea Scrolls in English*. New York: Penguin. von Franz, M. (1985). *Projection and Re-collection in Jungian Psychology*. London: Open Court Publishing.

Weber, M. (2002). *The Protestant Ethic and the Spirit of Capitalism: and Other Writings*. New York: Penguin Books.

Wells, H.G. (2004). *The Outline of History* (Vol. One). New York: Barnes and Noble.

Will, G. (2017). The presidency of Barack Obama brought America the presidency of Donald Trump. *National Review*.

Wiltgen, A., Adlera, H., Smith, R., Rufinoa, K., Fraziera, C., Shepard, C., Allena, J. (2015). Attachment insecurity and obsessive-compulsive personality disorder among inpatients with serious mental illness. *Journal of Affective Disorders, 174*, 411-415.

Winnicott, D. (1960). *The Maturational Process and the Facilitating Environment*. New York: International Universities Press.

Winnicott, D. (1966). Maternal Preoccupation. In P. Mariotti (Ed.), *Identification, Desire, and Transgenerational Issues*. East Sussex: Routledge.

Zukav, G. (2012). *The Dancing Wu-Li Masters*. New York: Random House.

INDEX

170, 171, 173, 176, 177, 178, 179,
182, 188, 197, 200, 201, 202, 203,
204, 205, 209, 210, 214, 215, 216,
220, 225, 230, 233, 234, 235, 236
obsessive-compulsive 69, 71
Ogden 58, 78
Omar 125
Orwell 87, 88, 214

P

paranoid 36, 58, 66, 72, 75, 87, 150
parenting 75, 78, 96, 104, 176, 177
passive-aggressive 78, 79
patriotism 199
Paul 22, 23, 44, 100, 101, 102, 113, 162, 233
perception 51, 63, 95, 96, 150
perfectionism 70, 75, 84, 88, 105, 137, 140, 141, 225
personality 15, 39, 55, 64, 66, 69, 70, 71, 72, 75, 80, 84, 91, 93, 94, 136
pessimistic 110
Peter Pan 58
Philo 154
Pinocchio 132
Plato 19, 20, 23, 162
pluralism 221
polite 72, 78, 79, 81
political correctness 35, 48, 55, 80, 81, 123, 133, 135, 141, 194, 199, 200, 207, 208, 210, 212, 213, 214, 215, 216, 222, 226, 230, 231, 232, 233
Pope Francis 103, 116
power 19, 23, 30, 31, 70, 86, 94, 95, 97, 101, 146, 149, 154, 162, 163, 165, 166, 182, 183, 203, 208, 210, 216, 218, 230, 232, 234
Princeton 198, 205

Progressivism 21, 34, 40, 95, 103, 106, 108, 110, 121, 124, 126, 128, 129, 135, 145, 147, 157, 163, 165, 169, 194, 195, 196, 202, 203, 208, 212, 223, 229, 235
projection 57, 58, 76, 84, 171
projective identification 78, 79
Prometheus 140
Protestants 103, 122, 138
psychoanalysis 44, 70, 110, 113, 137, 138, 160
psychology 27, 35, 41, 53, 56, 61, 64, 80, 106, 110, 112, 118, 138, 140, 143, 169, 179, 185, 200, 223
psychosis 16, 36, 66, 75, 87, 181
psychotherapy 75, 160
public schools 193, 196, 198, 199, 203

Q
Quran 217, 218

R
Rabbinic 105, 110, 113, 114, 115
racism 14, 34, 35, 38, 45, 49, 60, 87, 103, 110, 130, 132, 135, 157, 175, 185, 200, 230
rationalization 75, 159
Ratzinger 99, 114, 117, 239
Reagan 148
reality 10, 19, 58, 59, 60, 62, 63, 67, 114, 139, 145, 149, 151, 155, 157, 181, 197, 202, 227, 233
reflex 60
Reich 79, 131, 134, 235
religion 18, 29, 30, 37, 102, 106, 109, 110, 117, 118, 121, 125, 144, 145, 146, 162, 174, 218, 229, 233
repetition compulsion 39
Republican 20, 28, 136, 231
revolution 28, 188, 227

www.ingramcontent.com/pod-product-compliance
Lightning Source LLC
Chambersburg PA
CBHW052124270326
41930CB00012B/2754